THE BIBLE AS A DOCUMENT OF THE UNIVERSITY

SCHOLARS PRESS
POLEBRIDGE BOOKS

Number 3
The Bible as a Document of the University
Hans Dieter Betz, Editor

THE BIBLE AS A DOCUMENT OF THE UNIVERSITY

Edited by

Hans Dieter Betz

SCHOLARS PRESS

Distributed by
Scholars Press
101 Salem Street
Chico, CA 95926

The Bible as a Document of the University
Hans Dieter Betz, ed.

Ebeling, Gerhard, 1912–
    The Bible as a document of the university.

    (Polebridge books ; no. 3)
    Papers presented at the William Rainey Harper
Conference on Biblical Studies held at the University of
Chicago, Oct. 3–5, 1979.
    1. Bible—Criticism, interpretation,
etc.—Congresses. 2. Bible—Study—Congresses. 3.
Bible—Influence—Congresses. I. Barr, James, joint
author. II. Ricoeur, Paul, joint author. III. Betz, Hans
Dieter. IV. William Rainey Harper Conference on
Biblical Studies, University of Chicago, 1979. V. Title.
VI. Series.
BS511.2.E23   220'.07   80-23300
    ISBN 0-89130-421-5
    ISBN 0-89130-422-3 (pbk.)

Printed in the United States of America
1 2 3 4 5
Edwards Brothers, Inc.
Ann Arbor, Michigan 48106

TABLE OF CONTENTS

FOREWORD

Martin E. Marty
University of Chicago

This small book not only presents three essays of substance, but serves to introduce the Institute for the Advanced Study of Religion and its occasional publications to the public.

The Institute is located in Swift Hall, the home of the University of Chicago Divinity School whose work the Institute extends. From this location, the center relates advanced research in the Divinity School to work in progress at the University, in neighboring theological schools, and in other midwest centers — wherever serious concern for religion is pursued in the academy, church, or synagogue.

The activities of the Institute include: sponsoring conferences, lectures, and colloquies in the varied fields of religion and ministry; stimulating research and publication; providing hospitality for senior and research fellows from other campuses or ministries; and serving junior fellows who are in advanced dissertation-writing stages.

From time to time the Institute announces a project into which its constituents will be invited to pour their energies. We welcome inquiries about activities and suggestions for topics.

The inaugural celebration of the Institute occurred exactly one hundred years after William Rainey Harper, founding president of The University, first arrived in Chicago to take up teaching duties at the Baptist seminary, which was the antecedent to the Divinity School. Harper was a renowned biblical scholar, whose devotion to his field led to the conception of various journals and study centers. His imaginative placement of biblical studies in a number of places in The University is a testimony to his name and his intentions.

Because biblical studies remain integral and basic to any study of religion at any level and in order to honor Harper, the Institute opened in the autumn of 1979 with a major conference on the Bible. Several world-recognized scholars presented keynote, accent, and seminar addresses; three of their papers comprise the bulk of this volume. Their colleagues from Midwest schools spoke or responded at a number of seminars. The overflowing audiences included faculty, students, ministers, and interested non-specialists in general.

Many of the seminar papers were not designed to be published; they were informal, intended to provoke discussion, which most of them did quite effectively and generously. Other papers are committed to editors and publishers of journals and anthologies and will be available elsewhere in due course. Readers who are attracted by the material in this collection are advised to be in direct contact with those whose papers interest them. We are appending, for the reader's convenience, a program of the biblical conference. Everyone involved in the conference is indebted to the Lilly Endowment, whose generous assistance made the entire conference possible.

The conference had a number of accents. Its planners wanted participants to grapple with the ways in which the Bible remains a document of the university, the believing community, and the public culture. Professor Hans Dieter Betz, whose counsel was invaluable in planning and carrying out the conference, is well equipped to introduce the themes and to discuss their interrelation, their potential impact, and to suggest direction for those of us who now read these essays.

INTRODUCTION

Hans Dieter Betz
University of Chicago

"Ten years ago," said Martin Marty during the autumn 1979 conference on The Bible as a Document of the University, "such a conference could have been held in a phone booth." For whatever reasons, the intellectual and spiritual climate has now changed, and participation in the conference was substantial in both the number of participants and in the quality of the contributions.

The topic of the conference was chosen as a response to the new situation. The topic, "The Bible as a Document of the University," does not simply formulate a subject worth discussing, but also announces a distinct approach and an implied program for the study of the Bible at this particular time. Because this approach has been associated with the University of Chicago from the time of its first president, William Rainey Harper, the conference quite appropriately bore his name.

Indeed, approaching the Bible as a document of the university is not a new method purporting to solve problems which earlier methods failed to solve. In many ways it is an old method which has withstood many tests of time. Thus the conference of 1979 amounted to a reaffirmation of the valid and proven approach. On the other hand, approaching the Bible as document in a university context is far from simple conservatism since it welcomes constant revision and even revolution of methods, constant self-critical reflection about what we think we know, and never-ending inclusion of things previously unknown or which were deemed irrelevant.

At present the study of the Bible is quite visibly increasing in the number of its devotees. However, there are also frustrations and impediments: languages and methods must be mastered; the large volume of secondary literature must be worked through; and ancient texts display a general resistance to opening themselves to the modern intruder. All of this runs counter to current cultural trends toward gnostic immediacy of knowledge, an arrogant refusal to learn foreign languages, and the often lamented decline in literacy and interest in traditional religion.

On the other hand, since the study of the Bible is no longer a part of the dominant culture, it has all the promises of a counter-culture. There are endless resources to feed curious human minds, to engage their imagination, to come to terms with the questions and the possibilities of human existence, and to speak to the anxieties of conscience and heart.

The conference had thus a clearly formulated message: the Bible *is* a document of the university. But, does the Bible and its study legitimately belong in the university, and if so, why? And, what does the relationship of the Bible to the university imply?

The document called Bible is really an entire library of books coming from many centuries. Depending on the different Biblical canons in religious communities, the number of books to be included or excluded varies. These different canons have in the past been the origin of bitter hostilities first between Jews and Christians, then between Protestants and Catholics. In the religious world of today, however, they represent a real basis for new ecumenical encounters which go far beyond the limits drawn by hierarchies, councils, and administrations.

The function of the Bible in the university appears to be twofold. First, the Bible is recognized as a piece of world literature with a wide range of references to many disciplines. Second, the Bible is recognized sociologically as the holy scripture of living religious communities and traditions which exercise great influence in the contemporary society.

The two main papers of the conference address themselves to this double role of the Bible. Professor Gerhard Ebeling focuses on "The Bible as a Document of the University," and Professor James Barr directs his inquiry to "The Bible as a Document of Believing Communities." By complementing each other, the speakers have attempted to respond to the topic of the conference together rather than presenting alternative viewpoints.

The conference also took up and translated the issues into more specific problems in parallel seminars. These discussions were lively, generous, and often spontaneous, but (unfortunately) cannot be captured in a reasonable number of printed pages. Of the seminar papers which were read at the conference, only that of Professor Paul Ricoeur is reprinted here. Illness prevented Professor Ricoeur from attending the conference, and his paper arrived too late to receive sufficient study at that time. For this reason, and because his paper has the same general character as the two main papers, it was decided to include it here.

THE BIBLE AS A DOCUMENT OF THE UNIVERSITY

Gerhard Ebeling
University of Zürich

The great seal of the University of Tübingen has been in use since the establishment of that university in the year 1477./1/ The seal shows the figure of Jesus Christ standing on two books, the Old and the New Testament. In his left hand he carries the globe, and with his right hand he makes the gesture of teaching. The inscription on the ribbon surrounding him reads: *Ego sum via, veritas et vita*, "I am the way, the truth, and the life" (John 14, verse 6). All those who teach and learn at the university—this is what the symbol means—are subjects of him, Christ the true *magister*. By the same token he himself is the true doctrine, the standard of everything taught and learned. Accordingly, the Bible is accepted as the foundation and, in that sense, as the foundational document of the university.

Today this whole concept appears to be only an ancient relic, regarded with reverence but alien, distant and highly problematic. What did this concept once mean? Was it ever anything but mere ideology, an ideology that obscured the historically conditioned origins of the university and suppressed the truly scientific work done in that university? At any rate, the seal of the university of Tübingen does not express a unique concept. All other medieval universities shared this self-understanding. Whatever one may think of the concept today, it belongs inseparably with the origin of the university.

Yet it would certainly be absurd to derive the institution of the university simply from the Bible. Undoubtedly many far different factors were also at work when the universities of Bologna and Paris came into existence in the twelfth century. The same must be said about the triumphant proliferation of universities throughout Europe, which at the end of the Middle Ages was blessed with about 80 universities (Haskins, 1923:29), from France and England to Poland, and from Italy and Spain to Scandinavia. Despite all differences, however, all these institutions were united by their basically Christian character. Even when in the sixteenth century the European university was exported to all other parts of the world, including non-Christian cultures, the Christian character at first remained dominant. Then, because of the revolutionary changes which came with the modern era, the university separated itself more and more from its origins until today we might think that only the name *universitas* remains as a connecting link with the old university of the Middle Ages. The concept of the university has changed from the *universitas magistrorum et scholarium* to the *universitas litterarum*. The never ending quest for the "idea" of the university and the search for the spirit of the university also reveal the loss of its identity. No one today, however, would expect to receive any help from the Bible in that search for a new identity. On the contrary, the old role of the Bible in the history of the university is nowadays looked upon with suspicion. Nevertheless, the present dilemma with regard to the concept of the university invites us to ask again whether the symbolism of the university seal of Tübingen does not express a historically justified claim and even a permanent notion of truth.

I

The problem which we have raised is as old as Christendom itself. It is already manifest in Paul's antithesis of God's wisdom versus the wisdom of the world./2/ Later, Tertullian seems to have presented an early protest against a Christian university when he, a thousand years before its flourishing, radically separated what later found such an impressive institutional unity: "What indeed has Athens to do with Jerusalem? What concord is there between the Academy and the Church?" In Tertullian's view, they exclude each other just like heretics and Christians, like the curiosity of research and the simple-mindedness of faith. According to Tertullian it is the very principle of faith that there is nothing to look for beyond that faith./3/

But already Paul, and in his own way even Tertullian, were witnesses to the unavoidable contacts between the Christian faith and worldly scholarship, including the challenges presented by this relationship. Since then the entire history of the church, as well as European intellectual history, has been shaped by the struggle. In this struggle one party seeks a solution by trusting in the integration of revelation and reason, while the other party, in a suspicious and hostile tone, advocates their irreconcilable differences, be it for the sake of piety or for the sake of scientific integrity.

Despite all controversy, however, there are inescapable signs and clearly discernable reasons for the fact that fundamentally the Christian faith is both open to an intellectual culture and capable of opening people for it. At this point one should simply remember the enormous power of that faith which, quite uniquely in the history of religions, produced a highly reflective and methodologically organized theology. No less significant are the cultural achievements made by the church in the area of education. That these achievements are intimately related to the Christian faith is the result of the Bible. The authoritative role of the Bible in the Christian church makes high intellectual demands upon the readers, for the Bible is a book containing a library which encompasses two thousand years of history and has affected thousands of years more. It is a book at once deeply thoughtful and simple, so much so that it resembles the marvellous image of Gregory the Great: it is like a river which a lamb can cross on foot while an elephant must swim through it./4/ Divided into the Old and the New Testaments, it exists close to the borderline of contradiction, but at the same time points beyond itself to that which happened once and for all and to that which is to happen in the future. Full of demands and instructions, but primarily telling and proclaiming, the book intends to unite promise with commandment but also to distinguish between law and gospel. This book requires a special kind of reading: one must learn to read in the deeper sense of the term, and one must become ready for thinking in a responsible way. These demands, however, are the result not merely of the form of the Bible but also of its religious content.

If God and creation are clearly distinguished, people are free to comprehend the world and to deal with it in a secular way, in accordance with God's own handling of the world. Human beings are then free also to recognize all genuine wisdom, philosophy, and sciences, and to let them flourish. Moreover, if sinful humanity is reconciled with God, it is improper to strive for a utopian salvation of the world by spectacular achievements. Rather, the certainty of possessing true life enables the individual to look with soberness at the needs and the limitations of our temporal existence and to mobilize all powers, including those of the intellect, for service, so that love becomes the measure and standard for all human efforts. This is not a limitation of freedom but its fulfillment.

The fact that the university came into existence only during the peak of the Middle Ages, at first not through organizational planning but rather spontaneously, was made possible by a certain historical constellation which also nourished Christian impulses. During this period a real enthusiasm for learning broke loose. The cultural energies had been left idle and dormant too long in the historical soil. Buried remnants of the ancient heritage, especially Roman law and the works of Aristotle, gradually returned to light during the first period of the Renaissance./5/ When the feudal and clerical structure of the society began to change, the narrow framework of the monastic and cathedral schools also began to dissolve. The laity increasingly became the bearers of education, and the graduates developed into a new kind of aristocracy. Among the many factors at work in this development were, of course, the manifold forms of Christian engagement in the society, everything from the financial support of the universities out of church property and endowments, to the spiritual life-styles and clothing, to the priority of theology among the disciplines of learning.

When one looks for specifically Christian traits in the university as a whole, there are three such traits in which the Christian element expressed itself, though no doubt conditioned to a greater or lesser degree by the times. These three are universality, openness for diversity, and service to life.

The notion of universality does not depend primarily upon the concept of the *universitas* as an institution analogous to that of guild,/6/ but it depends upon the ecumenical nature of the *studium generale*. Regardless of nationality, anyone could belong to the university. Academic degrees granted the *licentia ubique docendi* ("the permission to teach at every place"). The basic forms of university organization and classroom procedures were more or less the same everywhere; scholarly languages were uniform in all places. The universal authorities of the occident, *sacerdotium* and *imperium* ("priesthood and kingdom"), recognized their responsibility for this third form of universality, the universities, and granted them the necessary privileges. Although as a place of scholarship it was an entity, the university, because of its origin, did in fact participate in that unity of the medieval society created by the Christian faith.

When I say that openness for diversity was another of the Christian traits of the university I mean that the medieval university, despite all the qualifications to be made, was not absolutely dominated by theology. In terms of size, the faculty of arts was by far the dominant one. In general, the faculty of jurisprudence, which, incidentally, also included canon law, enjoyed greater attendance than theology, which was not represented at all in some universities./7/ However, in cases of conflict with ecclesiastical doctrine, not only theologians but also members of the faculty of arts were censured. It must also be admitted that the discussions about heretical or non-Christian doctrines were mostly shadowboxing with predetermined results. Nevertheless, the differences between the schools of thought were anything but superficial. Moreover, theology as *sacra doctrina* understood itself to be fundamentally different from philosophy, that is, according to the language of the time, differed from the sciences governed by the *ratio*. But this did not mean that the rational sciences had no right to exist./8/ On the contrary, theology itself matured through its constant preoccupation with philosophy, a preoccupation which, in spite of all its grave shortcomings, was in part stimulated by the Christian faith's intentions to be different.

That service to life is a notion constitutive for the self-understanding of the medieval university is manifest in its structure of the disciplines. The formation of the arts according to the seven *artes liberales*, the *trivium* of the study of the language (grammar, rhetoric, and dialectic), and the *quadrivium* of the number sciences (arithmetic, geometry, music, and astronomy), is derived from antiquity. This structure was the vessel in which the early Middle Ages had preserved for the future the modest remnants of ancient learning. The basic scheme of study remained in force even when in following Aristotle the disciplines of physics, ethics, and metaphysics were added. None of all this, to be sure, was specifically Christian. The ancient division of the sciences was broken up, however, in the three faculties of higher education. Here the fundamental needs of human life became the priorities: the liberation from illness, the battle against injustice, and the salvation for eternal life. From these derive the vocations of the physician, the lawyer, and the clergyman. This vocational concept had no predecessor in antiquity. Even the common preparation for the vocations through the liberal arts had then to be understood as based upon the service to life and as the struggle against ignorance and foolishness. This new Christian motivation was expressed in an almost classic form in the charter of the university of Tübingen:

"So it is our good intention, in order to help dig the fountain of life, from which the ends of the world may draw inexhaustibly comforting and wholesome wisdom for the liberation from evil, for the protection against human stupidity and blindness, chosen and decided to found in our city of Tübingen a high common school and university . . ."/9/

What place, then, did the Bible itself occupy in this university? According to the scholastic concept of scholarship, the traditional authorities determined what was to be taught by all faculties. From these authorities one achieved the knowledge of the truth through the methods of concordance and exegesis. The Bible was only one of these authoritative books, and it functioned only in the curriculum of the theological faculty. Although theology was often simply called *sacra scriptura*, not even here was the Holy Scripture the only authority. While it was certainly the highest authority, the voice of the Church Fathers was present through the Biblical commentaries and other patristic writings. Prominent was the *Sentences* of Peter Lombard. His still rather simple system was then further developed in a highly subtle way by commentaries upon the *Sentences*, which contained an ever growing philosophical apparatus. The consequence of this scholarly enterprise was that the Bible, although highly revered, was prevented from stating its own message because of accommodations to the traditional doctrine of the church and the philosophical thought forms of the time. In the classroom the Bible ranked only second, while lecturing on the *Sentences* was considered to be of higher value.

Precisely at this point the Wittenberg Reformation began as a university reform./10/ Supported by the goals and the achievements of Humanism, Luther placed the Bible in the center of studies. Now, however, the Bible was interpreted according to its original languages, so that its own *modus loqueni* was brought out in contrast to its scholastic misrepresentation. This change had revolutionary consequences, not only in theology. Together with the far-reaching changes in the situation of the church and the consequent changes in the public and cultural life, all faculties were affected. Most notable was Melanchthon's humanistic reform of education which drastically changed the faculty of liberal arts./11/ But the role which the Bible was supposed to play in the new university curriculum was far from clear. There was no doubt the tendency to become biblicistic and legalistic. For the foundation of the first Protestant university in Marburg rather strange statutes were proposed but fortunately not adopted. It was proposed that the lectures in the liberal arts, especially in mathematics but no less in other faculties, should, under the threat of Anathema, be directed by the Word of God as the highest censor./12/

This proposal did not, however, conform to the Wittenberg Reformation and its understanding of Scripture. Rather, the Reformers' view was that the concentration upon the gospel would in principle free research and teaching. But the way to the actualization of this concept was long and was in the beginning blocked by the doctrinal battles of the so-called confessional era, when even the Bible was shackled and imprisoned by the orthodox dogmatics.

II

When one tries to evaluate the enormous changes in the situation of the universities which came with the modern era and its permanent revolutions in the sciences, one might be tempted to think in these rather simple terms: Things that were united since the beginning of the university have now become separated, at least in principle, even though inconsistently not separated in fact. Therefore, the Bible has really no place in the university. Only through its emancipation from the Bible has the university gained its autonomy and its true fulfillment. Such a view, however, is deceptive and can be easily disproved.

On the contrary, the Bible, just like any other historically and culturally important document, must never be eliminated from the university context. Moreover, the university itself should never pretend or believe that this institution is now completely sure of itself and based upon unshakable foundations. While keeping these points in mind, our discussion of the role of the Bible in the university must turn to a two-fold situation of crisis that characterizes our situation. As an object of research in the contemporary university the Bible, and especially its use in theology and the church, seem presently to be in a situation of crisis, a crisis that threatens to involve all of the theological enterprise. In addition, the university finds itself in a situation of crisis. Therefore, the question arises, at least for those who are interested in the Bible, whether these two crises have something to do with each other and whether some help can be expected from the study of the Bible in the university context. In the following we shall briefly discuss two aspects of the problem: the crisis of the Bible in the modern university, and the Bible in the crisis of the modern university.

1. If scientific discoveries are contradicted and critical thinking is suppressed in the name of the Bible, it never was and is not now the fault of the Bible but the fault of a theology that misunderstands and misuses it. Unfortunately, such abuses of the Bible still happen today. The well-known controversies with the natural sciences and the historical sciences, especially with regard to the Darwinian theory of evolution or the reliability of the Genesis stories of the origin of the universe, together with the miserable apologetic skirmishes of withdrawal after the lost battles, are certainly not pages of glory in the history of church and theology. That such things can happen even today, when public opinion would never give it any chance for success, is an indication of a small-minded and fearful faith which pretends to be strong but is really unfree. One should, for instance, recall that the official Prussian censorship under the repressive minister Wöllner attacked Immanuel Kant for his work on religion, objecting to what Wöllner called: "the perversion and degradation of many major and fundamental doctrines of Holy Scripture and Christianity"./13/ Wöllner also advised Kant to abstain from further publications of this kind. Such censorship must be called inappropriate, even if one agrees with Wöllner's judgment and even if one has the power to act as he did. Thus the principles of tolerance and academic freedom had to be fought for against the resistance of church and theology, a resistance that all too often was simply a pretext to cover up social and political interests. On the other hand, equally clear and easy to document is the fact that the Christian spirit often took an active part in the abolition of such false traditional power positions. Under quite different political circumstances in later totalitarian systems, Christian theologians often joined those who fought for freedom of conscience and academic freedom.

In spite of this historical evaluation it is easy to understand why theology has such great difficulties in the modern university, where even its right to exist is often questioned or denied. Even where theology is respectfully tolerated because of its traditional role, it has been moved to the periphery as one of the more dubious disciplines of study. A positivist or Marxist concept of knowledge was not the first to regard a discipline of study devoted to the Bible as without meaning. Already for German Idealism, which manifested itself in the widely celebrated establishment of the University of Berlin in the year 1810, theology was regarded as a dubious discipline. Yet Schleiermacher with his concept of theology was able to prevail against Fichte. In his proposal Fichte had demanded "a straight-forward public declaration" by a theological faculty, saying "that the will of God can be recognized without any special revelation and that those books" (namely the Biblical books, of which Fichte said contemptuously that they are written in an extremely dark language) "are by no means sources of knowledge but only a vehicle for public education. As such, the Biblical books are to be interpreted independently from what the authors should have said; the latter, however (that is, what they should have said) must be known prior to the interpretation on the basis of other sources of knowledge . . ."/14/

Indeed, the real decision about the Bible in the university is to be made not because of a position the university takes with regard to the Bible, but because of the position theology takes because of the Bible. This position should precisely not be the one recommended by Fichte, although theology has unfortunately all too often followed his line of thought voluntarily. The student of the Bible must rigorously and uncompromisingly determine what the authors of the Biblical books really did say. The student of the Bible must in no way know from prior external sources what those authors said or should have said. It is true that this scholarly approach is again and again caricatured by traditionalist piety as a form of slavery under the alien ideal of science and denigrated as profanation of the Holy Scripture. Such a scholarly approach, however, if applied consistently, does correspond to an attitude of true respect before the Biblical text. All available means of philological and historical criticism and of the arts of interpretation must be applied in order to bring out the original and uncorrupted meaning of the words in contrast to later deformations, prejudices, and layers of tradition. At this point, the demand of the university for scholarly integrity and the proper interest of theology in the meaning of the Biblical text converge.

To whatever extent one may lament the failures of modern theology, the achievements of Biblical scholarship are truly impressive, whether one thinks of textual criticism, the historical investigations of the canon, or the Life-of-Jesus research. In these areas of research, theology did not wait for criticism from the outside but by its own initiative achieved scientific breakthroughs which are recognized everywhere as scientifically exemplary. Also, the decision of the Reformers to have ministerial students attend universities for the primary reason of studying the Bible in that context has proven to be the right decision, in spite of all the setbacks due particularly to resistance by the churches to the historical-critical method. Without the challenge presented by existing within the university, theology and church would be helpless in confrontations with the modern world. But rigorous scientific accuracy is not simply dependent on its belonging to the university as institution, as if theology would be forced by that into doing things contradictory to its own intentions. Even if for some reason the theological discipline as a whole were to be expelled from the university, the subject matter of theology and its objectives would always demand the highest and most rigorous scientific standards. Part of this must certainly always be a hermeneutical self-criticism which prevents us from falling into mere routine performance, be it in the application of scholarly tools or in the employment of conventional categories of interpretation. Because of such degeneration the present widespread discontent about the performance of historical-critical scholarship is quite proper. Only when the crisis of the traditional understanding of the Bible is seriously faced can a better and more mature understanding emerge. The readiness to share responsibly the concerns of the Bible will prove to be not an obstruction but a new motivation to study theology scientifically.

One should add, however, that we must not underestimate the dire consequences for the study of the Bible if contacts with other disciplines of learning and the exchange of information should ever be impeded or cut off. But the reverse is equally true. The other disciplines of the university would also suffer a serious loss if the presence of theology in their midst should come to an end. The loss would not be that the Bible would no longer be available, but that the university would be left alone with it. Many disciplines in the university, to a greater or lesser extent, have continuous encounters with the Bible. The humanistic studies in particular confront the Bible in many ways. The Bible will always remain a highly important historical source, primarily of course for the history of religions, but also for the history of the ancient Near East, for Semitic, Greek, and Latin philology. Yet far more significant is the enormous impact of the Bible upon all areas of our culture. Whether one studies philosophy or literature, history of art, music, psychology, or sociology, everywhere one encounters the Bible, and then one must be familiar with it in order to understand the phenomena and interpret them. It may be true that for the ordinary person today the Bible has for the most part disappeared from consciousness. For the scholars in the university, however, the Bible continues to belong to their elementary education.

For the theologians it can only be beneficial, even though it may at times be uncomfortable, that scholarly preoccupation with the Bible is not their privilege alone. To be sure, even within the field of theology there are enough opportunities for a pluralism of viewpoints. There is really no reason to make fun of the existing confusion and the controversies. In which other scholarly disciplines are things really different? In fact, a wealth of historical and intellectual reflection is always a remarkable symptom of the great relevance of a historical phenomenon. This is true of the Bible in an unsurpassed way. There are not only the differences among individual scholars and between scholarly schools of thought and the influences of quite different traditions of religious piety. There are in addition the larger bodies of the Christian confessions and the fateful duality of the Jewish and Christian religions. All this diversity means two things at once: the amazingly manifold, often also perverted, impact of the Bible, and at the same time the demonstration of a genuine seriousness in the struggle for a true understanding of the Bible. If, therefore, extra-theological investigations which are based on other points of view and which have other interests enter the field, such correctives, if they prove to be valid, should be welcomed as opportunities and challenges for self-examination. In view of the significance of the Bible the limits of its investigation cannot be drawn widely enough!

For these reasons it would be completely unjustifiable if theology were ever to resign from interdisciplinary communication in the university. On the other hand, it would not be enough if the Bible were only treated as incidental by other disciplines. Observation and investigation of detailed matters cannot occur without an understanding of overarching connections. It is true that this is done to some extent by the discipline of the history of religions, but it goes without saying that this enormous field of study also needs to define foci for study. And it is by no means accidental that the most intensive concentration on Biblical studies (and within Biblical studies upon the few hundred pages of the New Testament) takes place wherever there is also the readiness to assume responsibility for the systematic-theological implications. One should not forget that the strongest impulse toward general *Religionswissenschaft* came from theology. Of course, the result was often the turning away from theology and its inner connections with Biblical religion. It would be short-sighted, however, to look toward religious homelessness or even the absence of religious commitment as the best presupposition for the understanding of religion.

The crisis of the Bible in the modern university—this expression sounds like degeneration and decline. Indeed, the modern university would never again take up the Bible as a theme in its official seal. On the other hand, the slogan of "crisis of the Bible in the university" revealed, as we have seen, nothing discouraging. Indeed, no one should be overly concerned because of the Bible. The Bible remains what it is, and in any case it can have only as much respect as it itself creates. To interpret this Bible under the changing conditions of the modern era will always be an intriguing and fascinating job for theology, in spite of all the crises which have to be faced again and again. It is also an impressive fact that the Bible continues to have its impact in the university quite apart from the discipline of theology. Admittedly, that fact is ambivalent. As a historical document the Bible is interesting in many different ways. For the problems of the university, however, it seems that the Bible has nothing to contribute, even though it meant so much for the university in the past.

2. The modern university is by no means lacking serious problems with regard to its own existence. Obviously, the modern university finds itself in a crisis situation, but it would be presumptuous even to try to analyze these problems within the confines of this paper. The complicated political and cultural situations within a global context and the controversial questions concerning the theories of science call for caution. On the other hand, we would be acting irresponsibly if we did not call attention to the open wounds of the modern university. It is precisely those ideas which are constitutive for the university and which present the most serious concerns: universality and unity, freedom, and the truth. A few remarks must suffice at this point, but all of us who live in university will remember our own experiences.

The universality and unity of the scientific disciplines has turned out to be only a phantom. When the christianized Aristotelianism of the old university disintegrated, the unimagined expansion and successes of the new sciences were made possible. Subsequently no other philosophy was able to succeed in this role of providing the unifying Weltanschauung, although some philosophical schools became temporarily and partially dominant. It is sobering to know that as early as the eighteenth century the idea was propagated to divide the university into separate trade-schools./15/ Even though nineteenth-century Idealism could not provide a lasting foundation, the university survived to the present. How can one still today justify the organizational unity of so many different branches of teaching and research under one roof? Is there a methodological justification, or is it mere pragmatism, or is it simply nostalgia? Is there at least a common and uniting climate of intellectual endeavor and scholarly ethos? There may be exceptional instances of this, but on the whole skepticism is well-founded. The avalanche of growth in the sciences and the ever-increasing specialization make exchange of information, even within the disciplines, increasingly difficult. Here and there we may find remnants of an *oecumene* of scholarship, cultivated perhaps in academies of sciences and learned congresses. But apart from these exceptions on the fringes, the daily life of the university presents a desolate picture of mass institutions, a picture which stands in stark contrast to the original concept of *universitas*.

The postulate of freedom has been connected with the university from its beginning. It was primarily academic freedom, a concept derived from the medieval *libertas*. It implied that freedom was a privilege and a reserved right. Among other things, exemption from taxes and separate jurisdiction were once part of that privilege. Even today, the university claims to possess the right of self-government, but this right is being continually reduced by governmental bureaucracies. Later came the demand for freedom to teach and to learn. Today this freedom is in serious danger not only from the outside but also from the inside, as many illustrations from the last ten years show. The freedom to teach and to learn is in danger especially when it loses its orientation. Freedom misunderstood as anarchy and falsely advertised by ideologies does not save the university from being enslaved by so-called social and political requirements and needs. How can even under the best circumstances the freedom to teach and to learn be exercised properly, and how can it be preserved? It is not to be forgotten that such freedom also includes the high degree of asceticism demanded by scholarly work, openness to self-criticism, readiness to be corrected again and again, the capacity to be unconditionally truthful and to be sincerely devoted to the search for truth.

The very concept of truth which seems so evidently part of any scientific enterprise is in danger of losing its home in the modern university and becoming literally a utopian idea. In the disciplines dealing primarily with language and interpretation, total relativism and agnosticism are widespread. In the so-called exact sciences truth no longer matters and only correct data are acceptable. The reason is that the notion of truth has an intrinsic relationship to human life, and precisely this relationship must be eliminated in modern scientific research. Still, however, such a relationship with human life is preserved in at least two forms: in the person of the scientist who conducts the research and in the unpredictable consequences of that research for the environment. Therefore, as soon as the questions of history and the social and cultural conditions of a discipline are raised, the competence of the scientist and the discipline are transcended. Also, we witness today how in all disciplines of the university ethical questions are raised, and together with them ultimately metaphysical and religious questions. Such questions transcend the competence of any given discipline, but they force the university again to take the relationship with life seriously as its ultimate criterion. A science which totally lacks such orientation toward life becomes dangerous to life.

In this crisis of the modern university the Bible is certainly a strange entity, but it is not alone; everything and everyone whose concern is with life as a whole appears similarly strange. Science does not produce life, but life always precedes science. It is useful to realize that without its embeddedness in life as a whole the scientific enterprise would have neither the stuff nor the breath of life. All the sciences and of course all the institutions of the university are embedded in life as it is actually lived by people. This life precedes, undergirds, and transcends the institutions, and they in turn depend on it. The Bible is also in this sense a document of the university because in this book life as it is lived by people has become manifest in an enormous condensation, so much so that from it time and again new impulses for life as it is lived emerge. This is not merely a dogmatic claim but a statement of fact.

Beyond this, let me make one further remark. I wish to make this remark as one who knows about the Bible as a source for life. There can be no doubt that the Bible is useless as a university statute. The Bible can only be of use to the university in its capacity as a completely different partner. Help for the crisis of the university cannot come from the drawing of borderlines for research or from putting on intellectual or spiritual shackles and fetters, but only from enabling people to exercise freedom, a freedom which releases the courage to pursue critical, and that means in the first place self-critical, scientific study. How can this happen? Someone who regards the universe as God's creation and humanity as reconciled with God is free from burdens of anxiety and has a clear vision of human reality as it is. Such a person has a sense of the universal unity of all things and is open and ready to perceive reality of whatever kind it may be and to listen and to discuss. Such a person is able to respect things that cannot be mediated or explained. Such a person has the freedom not to be ruthless in dealing with things or people. Truth as a liberating experience is also a safeguard against loss of orientation and perspective. In the final analysis, I submit, this truth is divine love which creates faith, which in turn creates human love. This truth evokes the freedom for human fulfillment in service./16/ With this I merely want to remind you of the things said at the beginning about the relationship between the Christian faith and learning as it was partially realized in the medieval university. In spite of all the changes since the Middle Ages, which of course cannot and should not be reversed, these basic facts of life remain true also today.

What I have said about the help the university can expect from the Bible is of course my own theological judgment. A study of the Bible in the university, which is open to all sides and aspects, will be the best whether my judgment is true or not. The goal of such studies, wherever in the university they are conducted, should be to find the real treasures buried there, to lift them up and to display them for all to see and to grasp.

NOTES

/1/ Decker-Hauff, 1977:47. See the picture and detailed description of the seal. "Zwischen den Wappenschilden Wirtemberg-Montbéliard und Tübingen steht, mächtig aufgereckt, der Heiland als Pantokrator, die Rechte lehrend erhoben, in der Linken die Weltkugel, um das Haupt einen Kreuz-Lilien-Nimbus. Vor der Brust schwebt die nimbierte Taube des Heiligen Geistes mit ausgebreiteten Schwingen. Christi rechter Fuss steht auf dem Neuen, sein linker auf dem Alten Testament. Das reichgeschlungene Schriftband führt den Text: + ego + sum + via + vita + et + veritas + (=Joh.14,6). Geistvoll durchdacht ist die Zuordnung der drei Begriffe Weg, Leben und Wahrheit zur Gestik der Gestalt: Neben der weisenden Rechte steht via, neben der die Welt haltenden Linken vita und zu beiden Seiten des Hauptes, gewissermassen vom Mund ausgehend, veritas. Das hervorragende Werk gehört wohl der Zeit um 1477 an."

/2/ 1 Cor 1–4.

/3/ De praescriptione haereticorum 7.9–13: Quid ergo Athenis et Hierosolymis? quid academiae et ecclesiae? quid haereticis et Christianis? nostra institutio de porticu Salomonis est, qui et ipse tradiderat dominum in simplicitate cordis esse quaerendum. uiderint qui Stoicum et Platonicum et dialecticum Christianismum protulerunt. nobis curiositate opus non est post Christum Iesum, nec inquisitione post euangelium. cum credimus, nihil desideramus ultra credere. hoc enim prius credimus, non esse, quod ultra credere debeamus.

/4/   Migne, vol. 75:515. Gregory the Great, *Moralium libri*, *Ep. ded.* cap. 4: Divinus . . . sermo sicut mysteriis prudentes exercet, sic plerumque superficie simplices refovet. Habet in publico unde parvulos nutriat, servat in secreto unde mentes sublimium in admiratione suspendat. Quasi quidam quippe est fluvius, ut ita dixerim, planus et altus, in quo et agnus ambulet, et elephas natet.

/5/   See Haskins (1923:7). "The occasion for the rise of the universities was a great revival of learning, not that revival of the fourteenth and fifteenth centuries to which the term is usually applied, but an earlier revival, less known though in its way quite as significant, which historians now call the renaissance of the twelfth century."

/6/   See Denifle (1956: 29ff.) and Haskins (1923: 13ff.).

/7/   See Rashdall (1936: vol. 1, 250 ff.).

/8/   See, e.g., Thomas Aquinas, *Summa Theologica*, I q. 1 a. 1 s.c.: Scriptura autem divinitus inspirata non pertinet ad philosophicas disciplinas, quae sunt secundum rationem humanam inventae. Utile igitur est, praeter philosophicas disciplinas, esse aliam scientiam divinitus inspiratam. ad 2: Unde nihil prohibet de eisdem rebus, de quibus philosophicae disciplinae tractant secundum quod sunt cognoscibilia lumine naturalis rationis, et aliam scientiam tractare secundum quod cognoscuntur lumine divinae revelationis. Unde theologia quae ad sacram doctrinam pertinet, differt secundum genus ab illa theologia quae pars philosophiae ponitur.

/9/   "Freiheitsbrief des Grafen Eberhard für die Universität Tübingen vom 9.Oktober 1477," in *Urkunden zur Geschichte der Universität Tübingen aus den Jahren 1476 bis 1550* (Tübingen 1877), P.31: "So haben wir in der guten meynung helffen zugraben den brunen des lebens darüs von allen enden der weltt vnersihlich geschöpfft mag werden trostlich und hailsam wyssheit zu erlöschung des verderplichen fürs Menschlicher vnuernunfft vnd Blintheit, vns vsserwelt vnd fürgenomen ain hoch gemain schul vnd Vniuersitet in unser stat Tüwingen zu stifften vnd vfftzurichten . . ."

/10/   See Bauer (1928) and Grane (1975).

/11/ See Hartfelder (1889, vol VII).

/12/ So the Church order of Hamburg of October 20, 1526, chapter
XXIX. Quia placuit Deo movere cor Principis nostri, ut nunc fulgente
Evangelii gloria universale studium apud Marpurgum erigere velit, idque
maxime necessarium sit, ut in Ecclesiis nostris multiplicentur, qui in
verbo et doctrina eisdem praesidere, ac quae recta sunt consulere possint:
Interdicimus in virtute Dei, ut nihil in ea legatur, quod negotiis regni Dei
obesse possit. In ea sint primum, qui sacras literas profiteantur, et id
quidem purissime, quoque deponantur. Deinde sint, qui Leges civiles
praelegant, sic tamen ut cautelae impiae Dei verbo circumcidantur, et
quae Dei verbo non conveniunt, per illud corrigantur. Idcirco vocentur
Jure Consulti docti simul et pii, qui sciant Dei verbum omnium doctri-
narum adhibere censorem, e quibus si quis nonnulla contra Dei verbum
adseruerit et suo ministerio et communione privetur. Tertio habeatur ad
minus unus Medicinae Professor, doctus simul et pius. Quarto praelegan-
tur artes liberales et politiores literae, adhibito in omnibus, praesertim in
Mathematicis, censore tutissimo, nempe sermone Dei. Quinto sint Profes-
sores Linguarum. Porro Jus illud contra fas vocatum Canonicum, omnino
legi prohibemus. Qui in hoc venerabili studio aliquid contra sanctum
verbum decernere ausus fuerti, anathema sit.

/13/ König (1970:47f): ". . . die Entstellung und Herabwürdigung man-
cher Haupt- und Grundlehren der heiligen Schrift und des Christentums."

/14/ Fichte (1960:57f): "Eine Schule des wissenschaftlichen Verstandesgebrauchs setzt voraus, dass verstanden und bis in seinen letzten Grund
durchdrungen werden könne, was sie sich aufgibt; sonach wäre ein
solches, das den Verstandesgebrauch sich verbittet und sich als ein
unbegreifliches Geheimnis gleich von vorn herein aufstellt, durch das
Wesen derselben von ihr ausgeschlossen. Wollte also etwa die Theologie
noch fernerhin auf einem Gotte bestehen, der etwas wollte ohne allen
Grund; welches Willens Inhalt kein Mensch durch sich selber begreifen,
sondern Gott selbst unmittelbar durch besondere Abgesandte ihm mitteil-
en müsste; dass eine solche Mitteilung geschehen sei und das Resultat
derselben in gewissen heiligen Büchern, die übrigens in einer sehr dun-
keln Sprache geschrieben sind, vorliege, von deren richtigem Verständ-
nisse die Seligkeit des Menschen abhange: so könnte wenigstens eine
Schule des Verstandesgebrauchs sich mit ihr nicht befassen. Nur wenn sie
diesen Anspruch auf ihr allein bekannte Geheimnisse und Zaubermittel
durch eine unumwundene Erklärung aufgibt, laut bekennend, dass der
Wille Gottes ohne alle besondere Offenbarung erkannt werden könne,
und dass jene Bücher durchaus nicht *Erkenntnisquelle*, sondern nur *Vehicu-
lum des Volksunterrichts* seien, welche, ganz unabhängig von dem, was die

Verfasser etwa wirklich gesagt haben, beim wirklichen Gebrauche also erklärt werden müssen, wie die Verfasser hätten sagen sollen; welches letztere, wie sie hätten sagen sollen, darum schon vor ihrer Erklärung anderwärts her bekannt sein müsse: nur unter dieser Bedingung kann der Stoff, den sie bisher besessen hat, von unserer Anstalt aufgenommen und jener Voraussetzung gemäss bearbeitet werden."

/15/ König (1970:17ff).

/16/ Ebeling (1979: vol. II, 417–26; Vol. III, 171–90).

WORKS CONSULTED

Bauer, Karl
 1928   *Die Wittenberger Universitätstheologie und die An- fänge der Deutschen Reformation.* Tübingen: Mohr.

Decker-Hauff, Hansmartin and Wilfred Setzler, eds.
 1977   *500 Jahre Eberhard-Karls-Universität Tübingen*, vol.3: *Die Universität Tübingen von 1477 bis 1977 in Bildern und Dokumenten.* Tübingen: Attempto.

Denifle, Heinrich
 1885   *Die Entstehung der Universitäten des Mittelalters bis 1400.* Graz: Akademische Druck -u. Verlaganstalt. Reprinted, 1956.

Ebeling, Gerhard
 1979   *Dogmatik des christlichen Glaubens.* Tübingen: Mohr.

Fichte, Johann Gottlieb
1960   "Deduzierter Plan einer zu Berlin zu errichten-
den höhern Lehranstalt, die in gehöriger Ver-
bindung mit einer Akademie der Wissenschaft-
en stehe," in Wilhelm Weischedel, ed., *Idee
und Wirklichkeit einer Universität. Dokumente zur
Geschichte der Friedrich-Wilhelms-Universität zu
Berlin*. Berlin: De Gruyter.

Grane, Leif
1975   "Modus loquendi theologicus. Luthers Kampf
um die Erneuerung der Theologie (1515–
1518)." *Acta Theologica Danica*. Leiden: Brill.

Hartfelder, Karl
1889   *Philipp Melanchthon als Praeceptor Germaniae,
Monumenta Germaniae Paedagogicae*, vol. VII.
Berlin: A. Hofmann and Co.

Haskins, Charles Homer
1923   *The Rise of Universities*. New York: Great Seal
Books.

Hildebrand, Bruno, ed.
1848   *Urkundensammlung über die Verfassung und Ver-
waltung der Universität Marburg unter Philip dem
Grossmüthigen*. Marburg: Elwert.

König, René
1970   *Vom Wesen der deutchen Universität*. Darmstadt:
Wissenschaftliche Buchges.

Migne, Jacques, ed.
n.d.   *Patrologia Latina*. Paris: Garnier Frères.

Rashdall, Hastings
1936   *The Universities of Europe in the Middle Ages*. A
New Edition in 3 vols. Ed. F.M. Powicke and
A. B. Emden. Oxford: Clarendon Press.

THE BIBLE AS A DOCUMENT
OF BELIEVING COMMUNITIES

James Barr

It is my honour and privilege to follow Professor Ebeling and, after having heard his profound analysis of what it means that the Bible is a document of the university, it is my task to speak of the Bible as a document of believing communities. The organic relationship of the Bible with believing communities is on the surface clear. The Bible takes its origin from within the life of believing communities; it is interpreted within the continuing life of these communities; the standard of its religious interpretation is the structure of faith which these communities maintain; and it has the task of providing a challenge, a force for innovation and a source of purification, to the life of these communities.

First of all we make two notes about the term "believing communities." The term "believing" is correct but is not entirely exact or comprehensive. For we have to think not only of Christianity but also of Judaism; and it is specifically within Christianity, and rather distinctively, that faith, the fact of believing, becomes the essential mark of the religious community—a fact marked by the enormously increased incidence of the Greek terms for "faith" and "believe" in the New Testament, as compared with the rather limited use of the Hebrew verb "believe" in the Hebrew Bible. Judaism, by contrast, is not so essentially a religion of belief: in Old Testament times it might be more accurate to designate it as having the fear of God as its essential motif—"fear" here has to be understood, not improperly as fright or terror, but properly as reverence and worship. And in post-biblical Judaism we might say that the essential is the keeping of the commandments rather than faith. Thus the term "believing" does not state exhaustively the character of the communities which are concerned religiously with the Bible. Again, not only in Judaism, but also in Christianity, have we to add at least two other central characteristics: these communities are worshipping communities, which address their prayers and praise to God; and they are practising communities, which seek to act socially and ethically in conformity with their understanding of God, in which understanding the guidance of scripture is an important element. Henceforth, when we speak of "believing" communities, it has to be understood that all these elements are included and implied.

Secondly, let us note the significance of the plural, "communities." That total community, which we may call the people of God, exists in actuality as a plurality. There is, first of all, the double manifestation of that people, as Israel and as the Church of Jesus Christ. Secondly, within the totality of the church, there is a diversity of communities. A community has to think and act as part of the whole church and with the whole church in mind. In this sense catholicity is an essential criterion for all valid Christian theology and thinking: the Christian has to think for the whole church and in the context of the church as a whole. But it is not realistic or practical to imagine that the entire church thinks as a unitary organism. It works and worships in particular communities, which may be defined and understood historically and sociologically. This was so even in the days of the "undivided church," as it is sometimes called: there were currents of Franciscan interpretation which differed from the currents of biblical interpretation among Dominicans or among the secular clergy. But, if it was so then, still more is it so now, since the Reformation and its sequel in Protestantism have brought so severe and so far-reaching a practical division of Christendom into separate bodies with their own traditions, their own confessional formulations and their own collective identities. In this sense the scripture is a document of each believing community in a slightly different way. But, yet more, the different denominations, with their varying interests and traditions in biblical interpretation, have since the later nineteenth century ceased to be the main bearers of identity for differing understandings of the Bible. Apart from the organized denominations, with their clearly delimited churches, creeds and clergy, there are also the more informal communities of biblical understanding, streams of consciousness transmitted by leaders, by books and periodicals, by conferences, by theological centres which emphasize a certain approach as against another. All or most of us belong, not only to a church, but to one of these trans-denominational currents, a vaguer but no less real sort of community. Existentialist interpretation, liberation theology, fundamentalism are all trends in biblical understanding that are carried and nourished by this more informal sort of community. These tendencies may often have a connection with particular denominational traditions but this is not *necessary*. Fundamentalism provides the most obvious example: the fundamentalist understanding of scripture forms a segment within many churches which themselves have a moderate or "catholic" majority. Conversely, the attempt to found and maintain a church which will keep strictly to pure fundamentalism seems doomed to disappointment, for there is no church, however extreme its conservatism, which does not harbour fears that some of its members, its ministers and its professors may be tainted with liberalism, no fundamentalist body or institution in which there is not some element of compromise, some minor concession perhaps to biblical criticism or some admission perhaps that mankind did not begin with a single man Adam. Thus the informal communities, the streams of understanding and biblical interpretation, are often only loosely related to the organized communities, the denominations. Yet even this loose relation remains very important. Existentialism has often had a loose linkage with Lutheranism, fundamentalism with confessional Protestantism, and so on. But we need go no farther with this at the moment: our point for the present is only to notice the plurality of the believing communities with which we are concerned, and also the plurality of the sorts and levels of believing communities.

Now in the Bible itself it was not much otherwise, and with this we come to the first main aspect of our subject. The Bible is in its origin a *product* of the believing community. Modern biblical study has made this much more plain to us than it could ever in the past have been. Traditional doctrines of scripture suggested to Christians over many centuries that the Bible was a message *from* God *to* the community. And of course we can still say this, but we can say it only more indirectly: in the sense, perhaps, that scripture grew out of the tradition of the believing community but, having so grown, became in its turn the Word of God to the community. And, as long as scripture was thought of as being something directly addressed *to* the community, attention was given primarily to the so-called writers, the persons who, inspired by God, wrote down the divine message in the books as we have them today, persons like Moses, Isaiah, St. Matthew, St. John. It was thought that their inspiration as writers of the sacred books was something that set them apart from other members of the community, indeed that their inspiration as writers of sacred books put them as writers in a different category from all that they did as members of the same community in other respects. Today we see all this differently. Scripture arose *out of* the traditions of the community. Certainly it *contained* various speeches made to the community by representatives of God, such as the prophets, who formed in a way the paradigm case for the idea of a Word of God addressed to the hearing people; and indeed in narrative passages it cited speeches literally made by God himself, or so depicted. But much of it, equally, was the community's address to God. It was Israel who sang the Psalms to God, not God who addressed them to Israel. God did not tell Israel how many kings there had been in the land of Edom (Gen. 36), nor did he have to intervene to tell them that Jehoshaphat began to reign over Judah in the fourth year of Ahab king of Israel (1 Kings 22.41); they knew this already, things of this kind were normal human information. And, more important, scripture was not created by a totally special act of God through a very small number of inspired writers. It came to be through the crystallization of the tradition of the people of God. Behind the persons who were traditonally represented by the designations "Moses," "Isaiah," "St. Matthew" and "St. John" there lie a great number of unnamed Israelites and Christians who received, maintained, restated and passed on the traditions which went to compose the eventual biblical books. Thus scripture was preceded by tradition and tradition came from the people of God, from the believing community.

This does not mean, however, that scripture is merely a transcript of what was average general opinion within the believing community. Neither in Israel nor in the early church did it work in this way. If it had been so, scripture would have included a good dose of Baalism from ancient Israel, and a good deal of Gnosticism from the early church. Even as it is, scripture contains a good deal more than is generally palatable that would later have been considered as unorthodox, and it certainly is not the case that scripture, either in the Old Testament or in the New, was the mouthpiece for a standard orthodoxy. The Bible is more like a battlefield, in which different traditions strive against one another: Deuteronomy's picture of Israel's destiny differs from Paul's own letters, St. John's Gospel gives a quite different picture of Jesus from that which any or all of the Synoptic Gospels gives. But, for all this difference of opinion within it, the Bible is not a mere collection of varying and contrary opinions that happened to be held. Rather, it is a graded and selected presentation from within the totality of ancient tradition of the people of God. It is not just all tradition, but certain leading and dominant traditions; and it is not just any person, but persons of leadership, approved and accepted in the believing communities. It is not just tradition as it happened to be, but tradition shaped and edited in such a way as to present *to* the believing community an adequate and necessary presentation of that tradition, as the older community wanted it to be known to the later community. In this sense it is a sort of canonical tradition. From this point of view the older idea, that scripture was something that came from God through his own appointed and inspired representatives and was given as an address *to* the community, was not so wrong after all. But the primary direction of movement is not from God to man, but from earlier to later.

Nevertheless the fact remained that the scripture had emerged from the tradition of the people of God. One of the peculiarities of scripture was that by the nature of its own formation it obscured its own earlier history. The effect of the existence of scripture was that almost all extra-scriptural tradition from the biblical period was forgotten. Scripture if read just as it stands conceals much or most of the development of tradition that has gone into its own making. It thus becomes possible to see scripture as a ball of mutually cohering and internally harmonious revelation, the historical growth of which is of secondary importance. In other words, some of the presuppositions of fundamentalism can easily be derived from the character which scripture, read in itself, can present. It has been the service of modern historical and critical reading of the Bible that scripture has been re-expanded into a far greater number of dimensions, and the stages of its growth and their relation to the ancient history of the believing communities have been made reaccessible to us. All this would not have been known, had historical criticism not been permitted to handle the Bible with all the rigour it could summon up.

Let us sum up one of the aspects of all this: we have seen that the traditional "Catholic" argument, that the Bible derived from the church, is entirely valid as against the traditional "Protestant" position which refused to see the Bible as deriving from the church and which therefore sought to give scripture priority over the church in the *ordo revelationis*. This Protestant view was basically an anachronism: it universalized, and gave permanent theological validity to, the relations which in the sixteenth and seventeenth centuries had seemed to be valid and important. The rightness of the "Catholic" argument in this respect, however, does not justify the way in which it was—in the older traditional and popular Catholicism—*used*. For it was used, as against Protestant thinking, to justify the relegation of scriptural authority to a secondary position and to assert the authority of the church through its magisterium to make authoritative decisions over the head of scripture itself. As against this sort of argumentation, the traditional Protestant position, that the scripture had authority over the believing community and that that authority could not be relativized through the interpretative authority of the church leadership, had at least a relative justification. We shall shortly see the reasons why this is so.

When we go back into biblical times themselves we find a situation quite different from that which the presence of a written scripture has created within Christianity. In an important sense the men of the Bible had no Bible. At least of the earlier stages this was true. When Abraham believed in the word spoken by God, there was no idea that this was something written down. When Paul came to believe that Jesus was risen from the dead, it was not because he had read about it in a true written account. The basic structures of belief, or of the fear of God, which are characteristic of the Bible, were created and believed before there was a Bible. In this sense biblical religion was not essentially a scripturally-based religion. It is only in the latter stages of the development, both within the Old Testament and within the New, that the category of scripture comes to dominate the life of the religion. When we today look at the life of ancient Israel, or at the life of the early church, under the heading of "biblical" or "scriptural" study, we are essentially taking up a position not within the biblical world but within the world of post-biblical religion. Especially in its narrative materials, which from many points of view were the core of biblical religion, the biblical period worked mainly not with written and therefore fixed texts, "scriptures," but with bodies of tradition that were still relatively fluid, which could be combined with other sources, subjected to redactional modification, and thus to some degree rewritten. Interpretation was not interpretation of a finished written text but rewriting, restatement, of an earlier theme. In Israel we can say with some probability that the first movement towards the placing of a written document at the centre of the religion came with the Deuteronomy, around the seventh century, in its conception of a written work known as "the law of Moses." In Christianity the first written documents were letters, and it was precisely because they were letters that they were written down, since it is of the nature of a letter that it must be written; but the fixation of the story of Jesus' life in the form a written Gospel comes only after one or two generations. Christianity was originally planted and spread without the existence of any full account of the story of Jesus such as our Gospels provide—at least, so far as we know. In these senses biblical religion was not a scriptural religion.

Now one or two objections against this account of the matter may be offered, and have to be considered. First, it may be pointed out, and with good reason, that the entire New Testament presupposed that there was already a scripture, and that the Old Testament provided the essential conceptuality for the New. Only in the terms already provided by the Old Testament was the mission and message of Jesus intelligible. /1/ And this is quite true. In itself, however, it is not in contradiction with what I have said. The conceptuality of the New Testament does not derive equally, evenly or exclusively from the Old. Part of the structure of the Old Testament religion is maintained, more or less unaltered, in the New: such for example is its monotheism, and its hatred of idolatry. Another part of the New Testament conceptuality came, however, not from the Old directly, but from the Jewish religion that followed the Old and the Jewish traditon of interpretation that developed from it. For instance, the stress on expectation of the Messiah, so central in the New Testament, goes considerably beyond what could be directly evidenced in the Old. And a third element of New Testament conceptuality belongs neither to the Old nor to the Judaism of the environment. The most striking such factor is the notion of incarnation itself. Thus, in spite of the quite essential place of the Old Testament in providing the intellectual background and the necessary presuppositions for the New, this did not work in such a way as to make the New Testament faith therein and thereby a scriptural religion, a faith essentially controlled and governed by the existence of a written scripture. If the authority of the Old Testament had been absolute and final, does it not irretrievably mean that the "Jews" of John 10.33 were in the right, and indeed only doing their duty, in stoning Jesus "because you, being a man, make yourself God"?

The same is true if we turn to the fact, often cited, that the Old Testament was an "authority" in the eyes of the New: *of course* it was authoritative, of course it was the Word of God, of course it was thought to give confirmation and the light of divine authorization to things that were said and done in New Testament times. Jesus died and rose again "according to the scriptures," things that happened were made luminous with the remark, "this is that which was spoken by the prophet, saying" or "that the Word of God might be fulfilled." Certainly in this sense there was already an authoritative scripture, and I have myself emphasized that this was soteriologically functional in the mission and meaning of Jesus, that he came into a world where there was already a scripture, and already an interpretation of that scripture, or rather many interpretations of it, within the people of God, the Jewish community of his time. /2/ All this is absolutely certain and entirely to be affirmed.

But it does not mean that the New Testament faith was thereby from the beginning designed or destined to be a scriptural religion in the same way in which the Old Testament had by that time become a scriptural religion. The core of the New Testament faith in its early days was not a written text or a scripture but the preaching of Jesus Christ crucified and risen. There is no indication that the production of a "New Testament" parallel in type or in authority to the Old was envisaged in the beginning. Jesus nowhere commanded that a written account of his deeds or sayings should be put down and nowhere did he sanction, much less command, the production of a New Testament. And, in spite of the full honour and authority ascribed to the Old Testament as the Word of God, it does not follow from this that early Christianity was thereby designed or understood to be a scriptural religion in the way in which the Old Testament religion, as seen not from within the early Old Testament situation itself but from within the perspectives of the first century A.D., was a scriptural religion. For the undoubted authority of the Old Testament and its undisputed status as Word of God did not mean for the men of the New Testament that it was the communicator of salvation, and in particular not the communicator of salvation for the Gentiles. Only the preaching of Jesus Christ as crucified and risen communicated salvation in the Christian sense. The Old Testament might well confirm and support that word of salvation, that message of salvation also included a quite critical look at the Old Testament and especially at the law of Moses. Thus, to sum up, it was by no means part of the agenda of the earliest Christianity that it should become a faith based on the Old Testament or at least on the Pentateuch. Only by hindsight, looking back upon the New Testament from post-biblical times, was it possible to take for granted an analogous relation: ancient Israel represented by its holy book the Old Testament, early Christianity similarly represented by its sacred book the New. Similarly, it is historically quite unlikely that the formation of a closed New Testament canon was originated and motivated by the consideration that, since an Old Testament canon already existed, therefore Christianity also should have something of the same sort. When in a late source of the New Testament, 2 Timothy 3:16, we first have explicit reference to the "inspiration" of "scripture," it is not plain whether Old or New Testament materials are meant (if indeed anyone then would have so classed them), or whether they included books now non-canonical or indeed any idea of canon at all; but most important of all is to see the function of this divinely-inspired scripture: there is no word of its historical accuracy, no word of its being the foundation of faith, no word of its being the central criterion for truth within Christianity. The scope of the inspiration of scripture is essentially *practical*: scripture is "profitable" (a very low-key word, strikingly contrasted with what has been made of this text in later times) for teaching, for correction, for training in righteousness, in order that the man of God may be complete and well equipped. In all these respects, then, New Testament Christianity was not a religion in which a Bible, a written scripture or group of texts, was a foremost category for the prime positive character of the faith. The essential word of life in New Testament Christianity was furnished not by written scripture but by the message of Jesus Christ crucified and risen, in other words by an oral tradition.

If all this is true of the category of "scripture," still more is it true of the category "canon." Contrary to some recent opinion, the category "canon" is not essential to the category "scripture." The idea of scripture requires that there should be certain sacred and authoritative writings, but it does not require that the compass, number and identity of these writings should be defined. To define them, and thus to create a closed collection separated from all other writings which are thus outside the canon, is to take up a position that had its origin long after the actual biblical times were over. In that later portion of the biblical period where scripture had begun to form at all, the central and major elements of scripture were clear and were well known; no one troubled about the status of the peripheral ones. Not only can it not be demonstrated that Christianity inherited a precise "canon" from the synagogue, /3/ but it may be wondered whether even the term "canon" is not an importation from later Christianity, imposed upon a Jewish situation where no such concept existed. What Hebrew expression exits for "canon"? Those phrases about certain books "making the hands unclean," which used to be taken as referring to a process of canonization, by no means certainly had this meaning. /4/ And, whether this is so or not, it is certain that the idea of canonicity plays no part in New Testament Christianity: nowhere in all the disputes between Jesus and the Jews, or between various currents in the New Testament church, does the question of whether this or that book is canonical have any function. Thus the idea of canonicity implies a way of seeing and defining problems from the perspective of a distinctly later Christianity.

If on the other hand we take the word "canon" in another sense, as the standard or basis for the life of the community and its interpretation of its written sources, then this is a function provided, within the early community, not by a list of accepted books but by the essential religious structure, by the fundamental faith of the believing community. The essential structure of faith is not something derived from the Bible, not something read off from it by subsequent study: on the contrary, it is generatively antecedent to the Bible; the faith is there, as the motive power of the tradition, before the creation of the biblical books. That structure of faith remains after a scripture is in existence, and theological interpretation of scripture works with this structure, arranging and ordering the biblical materials in relation to it. Thus the principal "canon" of theological interpretation in this sense is not the canon of scripture but something more like the *regula fidei*.

This however does not mean that the Bible should be seen as purely derivative, as a sort of secondary phenomenon in the total order of revelation. The formation of a fixed and written scripture, even if not primary, has momentous consequences for the total religious structure of both Judaism and Christianity. It might theoretically have been possible for the religions in question to continue on a basis of rolling verbal tradition, each age handing on to the next its own version of what the inherited religious substance had meant to it. /5/ This however is not the course that was in fact taken. The formation of scripture meant that continuing extra-scriptural tradition became in many ways basically exegetical: it might continue to have its own starting-points and its own content, but it already acknowledged as a matter of fact the now fixed scripture as an authority over against which it stood.

Why, however, was this so? What is there, or was there, about the Bible that made it so unquestionably central, so inevitable and necessary, so sufficient and so authoritative? What was there in it that, though it had grown from the- tradition of the people of God, made it in rank superior to all future traditions of that same people? Perhaps the basic reason lies in the literary character of the Bible as the expression of the life, the experience, the thinking of the people of God. Though it contains doctrine or theology, though—as we have said—it requires a doctrinal structure to enable us to understand it theologically, and though the movement of doctrinal or theological thinking is a motif that runs through the Bible and supports its chronological sequences, the Bible is not in itself a work of doctrine or of theology. As all of us know, those who have sought to state within one or two volumes what is the theology of the Old Testament or the theology of the New—to say nothing of the theology of the Bible as a whole—have found it a very difficult thing to do, and even more difficult to obtain the assent of others to the product when they have done it. In a sense—surprising as it seems to say it—the Bible, or most of it, is not concerned to enunciate ultimate truth. Its concern is more with something contingent. It furnishes us with the *classic* literary expression of the people of God's experience in their contact with God. Interlaced as the whole is with theology, theology or doctrine is not the prime form in which it speaks. It speaks rather in the voice of a people's hymns in praise of its God, in the moral instructions and counsels of its teachers, in the utterances of prophets for such or such a time, in letters and occasional papers, but most of all, of course, in narrative. Narrative story is, as has been so widely recognized, the most typical of all the Bible's literary forms (Barr, 1976: 1–17). It is in these forms, rather than in direct doctrinal formulation or theological precision, that biblical faith expressed itself. Its range of literary form, of emotional appeal, of personal communication, was very much greater than that of the most correct and purest of doctrine. Thus, because it comes from and expresses a much wider range of human experience and questioning, the Bible speaks to and for a much wider range of experience and questioning than does any doctrinal formulation, however otherwise accurate. For this reason the Bible is uniquely qualified to be the preaching base of the church, the locus of the main group of texts that have to be studied, pondered, expounded and interpreted in it; and this is equally the reason why it is the primary source of the language of prayer and liturgy.

Moreover, the Bible represents a range and variety of viewpoints that no doctrinal position has ever been able to incorporate or to represent. No matter how "biblical" a theology seeks to be, it finds the biblical material resisting its constructions and failing to conform to its alignments. How completely, for instance, does the Jesus of the Gospels fail to present himself in terms that fit with the classical trinitarian/incarnational doctrine! But when we try to produce a "Jesus of history" who is free from all traces of this doctrine, we find that this does not seem to work either. And in the mid-twentieth century, when the most sophisticated attempt was made to produce a "really" biblical theology, built upon certain linguistic indexes understood to be pointers to an underlying biblical logic, this in the end turned out not to fit with the biblical text either. Thus, we may say, this intransigence of the Bible is something that has to be accepted and lived with. A major positive function of the Bible is to challenge the doctrinal and theological systems which so quickly and so powerfully come to control people's thinking about God. It was a major aspect of the Protestant Reformation that it sought to liberate scripture from its bondage to traditional doctrine; and this was a correct insight. But of course, as manifold experience has shown, Protestantism is fully as capable as was medieval Catholicism of imprisoning the variety of the biblical message within a rigid doctrinal system. Indeed, the fact that Protestant doctrinal systems often claim to be more exclusively biblical, and reject the manifoldness of a theology which admits other sources of authority, only makes these systems even more imprisoning.

It is therefore of vital importance that the primary place in the preaching and therefore in the thinking and meditation of the community should be taken by careful and detailed interpretation of scripture, in which a genuine attempt is made to discover and interpret what it really means, as against our antecedent expectation of what it ought to mean. To some, perhaps, this warning may seem to be unnecessary: is not most preaching in some sense related to biblical texts? Well, I don't think it is; and such things as topical preaching, preaching from general theological questions of the present day, and—most common of all—the mere rehearsal of accepted and traditional religious beliefs, attached to some text or other (a procedure most marked among those who actually give the highest place to the "doctrine of scripture")—all of these things should have at most a limited place, and first place should be given to the search for the meaning of scripture itself; this is what the community needs, and wants, to hear.

But here we have to make a cross-reference to Dr. Ebeling's subject and say something about the Bible as a document, not so much technically of the university, but at least of academic study in the academic world which lies beyond the religious community itself. Of that academic world the university is the most prominent organized manifestation. The effectiveness of the Bible as a document of the believing community is related to the extent to which the study of it is shared by the believing community with the academic world. It is in the interest of the believing community itself that it should not too jealously insist on keeping the interpretation of scripture, and indeed theological education altogether, within the control of the church or other religious community, but must be opened to comment and discussion from any competently informed quarter. Unless this is done, the Bible will be imprisoned in the categories of the present religious community and will cease to have any new message to deliver. And the idea that a document of faith can be interpreted only from within faith is an impossibly solipsistic position: carried to its logical conclusion, it could only mean that no one could say anything about any ideological position which he himself did not share. The ability of the Bible to speak afresh to men of faith and to the community of believers is in part dependent on the openness of that faith to insights and arguments that come from beyond itself.

But we must return to our main point under consideration here: have we given sufficient reasons why the Bible continues to have a quite unique sort of authority, a kind of function quite different from those of other power instances within the believing community? Why, after all, the Bible more than other books, and why it more than other observations about life, history and science which may be equally true and more relevant to us in our society? What is special about the Bible? Is it the time when it was written, or the peculiar nature of its contents? Or is it the sheer contingent fact that the church at an earlier stage decided that this was its scripture, so that we cannot get away from it today even if we wanted to do so?

Any answer to these questions must have several parts. Perhaps we might begin with the notion of inspiration, which was long traditional in both Catholic and Protestant theology but became discredited through its association with fundamentalism. Inspiration today can no longer mean historical accuracy or any sort of infallibility, nor can it be restricted to the mere writing down of scripture by its supposed "writers." As we have seen, the communication and formation of what we now know as the Bible must extend over an enormous number of people, most of them anonymous. It must mean the inspiration not of writers of books, but of the tradition of the believing community, out of which scripture was eventually formed. It must mean that God was with his people in ancient times, in his Spirit, so that their responses to him were in adequate measure true and valid responses, which thus formed some sort of index to his nature and activity. "Adequate" is as far as we can go in this, for the Bible is not theologically perfect any more than it is necessarily historically accurate.

This inspiration thus takes place in a history, the history of Israel and of the ancient church. It is thus the history of a people: inspiration is not the inspiration of books, but the inspiration of the people from whom the books came. Is inspiration then a special event, an influence or relationship, which once existed but no longer exists? I think not. The relationship through which God is with his people in his Spirit in the formation of their life and tradition is not essentially different in kind from the mode in which he is with his people today. But the factual formation of scripture, and the consequent result that new tradition formation no longer becomes scripture, but has exegetical character as interpretation of an ancient scripture, separates the effects of that same inspiration from the effects which it had when scripture was still in process of being created. It is thus possible to say that the relationship which we call, or may call, by the name inspiration is a relation that is constant throughout history, but nevertheless to allow that the actual production of scripture is a once-for-all effect of that relationship.

And as we have just said, the process of inspiration is located in a history and is thus historical in character. The history in question is the history of the believing community and their traditions. That is to say, it is not identical with the story which the Bible narrates; rather, it is the history that lies behind the materials of the Bible, the history that the Bible as a text often conceals, the history of the Deuteronomists and the redactors of the prophetic books, the history of the interpretations of Jesus in and behind the various gospels. In this sense, through the historical character of its origin, the Bible recalls the believing community to its origins; it suggests that the way in which these men of older times reacted to their problems can be and should be suggestive and rich in paradigmatic guidance for us when we face the problems of the community today.

Nevertheless there is a displacement between the location of the idea of scriptural inspiration and the historical rootage of the Christian faith itself. The faith is not itself founded upon the Bible or upon biblical inspiration; it is founded upon persons of the past, especially of course Jesus Christ, and upon what they said and did. The Bible is the primary source for these persons and events, and yet it is not an exact transcript of what they were or what they said. The reality of the resurrection does not depend on the accuracy of the reports of that complex of events. Indeed, it depends rather on the inaccuracy of these reports, since if they were quite accurate they would contradict one another. Faith is a personal relation to God through Jesus Christ, and the dealing with biblical texts is one part of the total functioning of faith in relation to God. The true believer is a believer in God and in Christ, not in the first place a believer in the Bible.

This historical aspect of Christian faith is linked with one of the obvious features of the Bible which has already been mentioned, namely the centrality of narrative in its literary form, especially in the long story from Genesis to the end of Kings in the Old Testament and in the Gospels and Acts in the New. The story is not a collection of tales which might have happened at any time; it is a canonical story, a sort of foundation story. Starting from the beginnings of the world, it runs down to a certain point where some kind of decisive or satisfactory stage is reached, at which the story stops; history goes on, but the story falls more and more into the past. For the Samaritans it stopped more or less at the point where Israel entered Canaan and was close to Shechem; for the Jews it had another major stage which ended with the promise-like sign of hope, the lifting up of the head of the exiled Jehoiachin by Amel-Marduk king of Babylon in the thirty-seventh year of his exile. For Christians, taking a new departure with the coming of Jesus, it ended just after the resurrection, or, for St. Luke, with the arrival of St. Paul in Rome. This narrative material, basically story but including many historical elements, is highly characteristic of the Bible. This concept of a canonical story is much more important for the nature of scripture than is the canon of scripture, in the sense of a definition of the list of sacred books, and is of course very much earlier.

But the importance and the value of this entire historical aspect become distorted if it is too exclusively emphasized. The function of the Bible in the believing community is not in essence that of providing true information about the past, or even of providing true theological interpretations of past events, of past revelation. It is equally true and equally characteristic that the Bible looks towards the future. Its function is not to bring memories from ancient times, which have then to be reinterpreted to make them relevant for today, but to provide paradigms in which the life of a later time, i.e., future from the viewpoint of the texts themselves, may be illuminated. This is true not only of those passages, traditionally deemed "prophetic," which seem to have a literal purport in the future, but also of many passages which seem to have their primary references in the past, i.e., many narrative passages. The function of the Old Testament in relation to the mission of Jesus is that it provided the conceptuality in which his work could be intelligible; that is, that which was written long ago now made luminous the sayings and events of today and gave lineaments to hope for the future that still lay ahead. In this sense it still works today and this is why it functions creatively in the preaching and meditation of the believing community. A story of Abraham, for instance, may have been told originally not in order to give exact information about situations of the second millennium B.C., but to convey patterns of hope borne by the figure of the man who had recieved the promise of God; this is how this same story can and should still function today. The narratives of Jesus are not there only to tell what he historically said and did. They are there also to furnish visions of the present and future life of the one who lives after death and who will come in the end as judge. The Gospels often tell, not of the past Jesus, but of the future Jesus; when this is so they do not, and cannot, speak with historical accuracy.

The perception of the future emphasis of biblical interpretation has often been obscured because it has been linked with an absurd literalism in reference to future predictions, coupled with a hard fundamentalism about past narrative—exactly the wrong emphasis, for it is the past narrative that is the primary carrier of future illumination in the Bible, so that its accuracy concerning past history is not relevant to its function in this respect. But in spite of these well-known distortions, which have made chiliastic and millenarian views rightly suspected by all sensible believers, the future direction of scripture is of fundamental importance for the believing community. But the future direction of scripture can be rightly realized and exploited only in conjunction with its past references, for it is the past references that, though historically imprecise, provide the historically-given definitions of its terms. And here again we have a reason why the Bible has to be understood with a fully historical understanding, aligned with disciplines lying outside the biblical and theological fields: only that can guard us from systematic misunderstanding of the range of possible meanings of biblical terms in their reference to present and future.

These, then, are various ways in which the Bible, though historically derivative from the life and tradition of the believing community, can and must function as a prime and controlling paradigm within the continuing life and understanding of that community. And before we go farther from this point it will be good to add some remarks about the relation of the Old Testament to the new and the consequent structural differences between Judaism and Christianity.

Certain modern currents, in these times in which hermeneutics have been so fashionable, have tended to suggest that the New Testament stands in an essentially hermeneutic relation to the Old: the Old is already there, and the New Testament interprets it. I think this is an error. Of course the New Testament does provide interpretations of Old Testament materials; but its *essence* is not that it provides interpretations of the Old Testament, its essence is that there is a new *substance* there, the substance of the coming of Jesus, his teaching, his life, death and resurrection, his meaning. It is this new substance — though linked to the Old Testament with chains of meaning, nevertheless a new substance — that is the theme of the New Testament. Now this means that a Christian interpretation of the Old Testament will not necessarily conflict with a Jewish interpretation of the same; they may differ, it is very likely that they will differ, but they do not in principle require to be in conflict. In fact important elements of Jewish exegesis of the Old Testament have at various times filtered into the tradition of Christian understanding. The two most important such periods have been, first, the Reformation period, when the heritage of medieval Jewish exegesis was fruitful in Protestant exegesis, and, secondly, the mid-twentieth century, with the substantial positive gains made through Jewish scholarship in North America, in Israel, and elsewhere, and made available for Christian understanding everywhere. Where Judaism and Christianity differ basically is not over their understanding of the Old Testament but over their understanding of what was going on in that new substance which is peculiar to the New. The core of Christianity lies in its interpretation of that new substance. Judaism, on the other hand, does not provide an official interpretation of that substance, but clearly if unofficially rejects it.

This has an effect on one side-question concerning the canon. It has been suggested that the use by the church of the "Hebrew canon" of the Old Testament is of great significance, because it means that church and synagogue thereby have the same basic Bible. /6/ This, I think, is mistaken. The question of whether the church follows the Hebrew canon or the canon — if it is a canon — of the traditional Septuagint is of only minor significance for relations between church and synagogue. The fact that the basic distinctive scripture of the church is the New Testament sets it so

widely apart from the synagogue that questions of the margin of
the Old Testament canon are quite insignificant in comparison.

But this leads to a more profound question. I have already
implied that the two major entities with which we have to deal are
Bible and doctrine or Bible and theology. But this is not absolutely
correct, for it applies to Christianity rather than to Judaism.
Though we have made clear that the fundamental form of scripture is not theology or doctrine, it is a basic characteristic of
Christianity that it generates theology. In spite of the intense
irritation that theology, especially active theology, stimulates in
people it has proved impossible to get away from the theology-
generating character of Christianity. One central reason for this, we
may suggest, is its possession of a sort of double scripture in Old
and New Testaments. The relations between these two generate
some of the most fundamental and historically earliest questions of
Christian theology, and they were questions that could not be
answered except by true theological thinking. In Judaism nothing
quite of this kind took place. The activity within Judaism which
fulfilled a similar function to that of theology within Christianity is
law. It could hardly be disputed that in Judaism law is a much
more prominent sort of activity than theology is. But this agrees
with the fact that the relation of law to authoritative sources in
Judaism is quite different from the relation of theology to scripture
in Christianity; and this again reflects back on the canon question,
not so much on the formal definition of the canon but on the way
in which the actual sources are interrelated. For Jewish law the real
canonical document is the Torah, and beside it the other parts of
the biblical canon are quite subsidiary; but alongside the Torah
there is from an early date the recognition of the oral tradition of
law, and the elaboration of discussions of this oral tradition,
eventually collected in the Mishnah and Talmud, though not
termed "canonical" or "biblical," assumed by scripture, in relation
to theology, in Christianity.

Returning to Christianity, it is a characteristic then of this
faith that it produces questions which generate theology, questions
which cannot be properly dealt with by the faith-inspired utterances of scripture but press for consideration under the more
deliberate, more disciplined, more conscious and perhaps even
more abstract process that is theology. The most important of such
questions, of course, is that of the relationship between Jesus
Christ and God the Father. Such questions cannot be answered
purely by reading off from the data of scripture. But they can be

answered satisfactorily only in so far as the answers suggested provide a framework within which scripture can be expounded in a way that conforms to its actual text and also brings out its own inner intentions.

But the involvement of the believing community in scripture cannot be measured in terms of theology alone, or perhaps we should say that theology must be seen in its ethical dimension as well as in its doctrinal dimension. The community, as I remarked at the beginning, is a practising community; it has to order its life and actions within the context of society and the total world. This is the *ethical* dimension of the community's involvement with the Bible. Perhaps it can be said that on this side the believing community today is more uncertain of its relations to the Bible than is the case on the dogmatic or theological side. Does the Bible really lay down rules for marriage and divorce in modern society? Can the command "thou shalt not kill" be reasonably understood as implying a prohibition of abortion? Does the Bible provide guidance for questions of peace and war? Is the perspective of liberty and liberation in the Bible a valid grounding for the ideas of modern liberation theologies? Conversely, is it not the case through much of Christian history that the Bible, taken as guidance, has been used to justify all sorts of unjust and socially oppressive practices? Are communities not in a cleft stick in their appeal to the Bible—either respecting its social precisions too much, and thus enforcing on a modern society what appear to be the social norms of an ancient time, or else spiritualizing the sayings so much that they lose all their concrete reality?

Here again we must draw a distinction between Judaism and Christianity. In Judaism the community remains univocally related to the Torah, and the working out of the religion in terms of Jewish law is an absolute first priority of the society. The relation of the Torah to practice, or at least to some departments of practice which are traditionally defined and organized, is thus built into the main structure of the religion in such a way that if this were not there the religion would have broken down. In Christianity it is otherwise. For one thing, Christianity on its ethical side has to face a difficult dialectic between Old and New Testaments. Although it has always been clear that at least some aspects of Old Testament social behavior were not to be valid or authoritative within Christianity, it remains true that over much of the history of Christendom it has been from the Old Testament side rather than from that of the New that Christian social and political thinking has drawn its norms and its paradigms. /7/ While the perspective of the Old Testament was for the most part the society of Israel, one particular people, that of the New was rather a society that coincided with no national unit but was universal, spread throughout all nations yet comprising only a minority in each. The result of the consequent difficulties has been a much more splintered and uneven use of biblical material in ethical questions within Christianity than has been found in questions of practice within Judaism.

Perhaps we have to accept that, seen from within Christianity, the Bible offers a wide variety of paradigms for the understanding of ethics and the taking of decisions in practice. One which has been historically most powerful, and has lasted throughout much of traditional Christendom, could be called the theocratic paradigm: according to it all the essential structures of human society had been laid down by God, and the believing community had the task of accepting this and telling others so. In the nineteenth century and the twentieth the prophetic paradigm came to the fore: the believing community should speak out like a prophet against the injustices of society. According to this paradigm theocratic legitimacy was of no ultimate value in the eyes of God; unless it delivered the goods in the form of social justice God himself would sweep it away. Today we hear more of a paradigm centred upon liberation; and yet another is an essentially eschatological paradigm, based on the biblical hope for a new world in which righteousness and peace will dwell, but seeing that hope as having some common substance with Marxism. The conflict between these paradigms is part of the existence of the believing community. When we hear, for example, that some want the churches to give financial support to fighters against the existing order in this or that part of the world, and others oppose this idea, we are witnessing the conflict of these paradigms in the life of the community. And it is not easy to resolve the conflict by saying that such and such a paradigm is a false one, having no basis in the Bible or in the religion of the community, for it seems likely that the Bible does in fact furnish several possible paradigms, all of which must play upon the conscience and thinking of the community if justice is to be done and peace maintained. In other words, it may not be our task to remove the conflict by ruling out certain paradigms as totally illegitimate (though there may indeed be some suggested paradigms of which this is the case), or to neutralize it by seeking to set up a fixed and final order of priority between them. In this sense it may be—and here I follow something I once heard from Erich Dinkler—that there is no one Christian ethic:

that from the Gospel you can go in more than one direction. You can go, for instance, in a more socialistic direction, but you can also go in a more conservative direction; you can go in a more libertarian direction, but you can also go in a more realistic, more restrictive direction. Christian faith in itself does not provide a simple, direct and overriding decision between several such pairs of possibilities.

Within the believing community, ethical questions cannot be given timeless, eternal solutions. They are related not only to the Bible but also to the situation in which people find themselves. The suffering of people in difficulty, the factual problems of the poor, the restriction of freedom in thought and expression, the psychological tension brought about by existing social arrangements: all these are criteria for Christian social perception and decision as much as are principles, ideologies and even the words of the Bible itself.

The problem for the believing community is to achieve openness to all that is relevant in this. The Bible itself, seen rightly, offers a great width of vision. It has numerous paradigms of social concern and action; it is not the expression in a narrow sense of any one theology or ideology; it contains a certain amount of advice and instruction that was general human property, held in common with ancient Egypt or ancient Greece. It gives a picture of the world as a place within which a man may move. But it has to be confessed that at times the Bible has become more of a prison for mankind, a force that restricted vision, prevented change, and limited the possibilities of both faith and action. The believing community is a sort of clearing house of information and understanding: if it has the material of holy scripture, it must bring and set against it the knowledge of man's social and personal problems today. Openness to the world is gained for the Bible when the study and appreciation of it, as I have emphasized, are not limited by the traditional perceptions and methods of the believing community but are opened to all the world and to its ways of thinking. And with this, starting out from the believing community, we come back to join hands with the thought of the Bible as the document of the university, of which Professor Ebeling has so finely spoken, and to which the University of Chicago, not least through its first President, William Rainey Harper, has so nobly witnessed.

NOTES

/1/ I have discussed the ramifications of this in my books, Barr (1966) and (1973), especially in the former.

/2/ This position is central to my two books referred to in note /1/ above.

/3/ Sundberg (1976:137).

/4/ It may be that the passages should be interpreted as meaning exactly what they say: i.e., the question is not of canonicity, but of the *ritual effect* of handling the documents.

/5/ See for instance Evans (1971) and Barr (1973).

/6/ E.g. Childs (1979:666): "In order to maintain a common scripture with Judaism." For the idea that the Old Testament of the church must be the Greek rather than the Hebrew text, see recently Barthélemy (1978:111–39).

/7/ On this and the following material, see the writer's article, "The Bible as a Political Document," forthcoming in the *Bulletin of the John Rylands University Library*, Manchester.

WORKS CONSULTED

Barr, James
    1966   *Old and New in Interpretation*. London: SCM Press; and New York: Harper and Row.

    1973   *The Bible in the Modern World*. London: SCM Press; New York: Harper and Row.

1976   "Story and History in Biblical Theology," *The Journal of Religion* 56:1–17.

Barthélemy, D.
1978   *Études d'histoire du texte de l'Ancien Testament.* Fribourg: Éditions Universitaires.

Childs, B.S.
1979   *Introduction to the Old Testament as Scripture.* London: SCM Press.

Evans, C.F.
1971   *Is 'Holy Scripture' Christian?* London: SCM Press.

Sundberg, A.C.
1976   Article in *The Interpreters Dictionary of the Bible*, Supplementary Volume. Nashville: Abingdon.

THE BIBLE AND THE IMAGINATION*

Paul Ricoeur

I. Presuppositions

1. When Dean Kitagawa proposed the topic "The Bible and the Imagination" to me, I was first perplexed, then intrigued, and finally fascinated by this subject. The title is, indeed, baffling, even paradoxical. Is not the imagination, by common consent, a faculty of free invention, therefore something not governed by rules, something wild and untamed? What is more, is it not condemned to wandering about the internal spaces of what we conventionally call the mental kingdom, and does it not therefore lack any referential import, being entirely disconnected from what is really real? As for the Bible, is it not a closed book, one whose meaning is fixed forever and therefore the enemy of any radically original creation of meaning? Does it not claim to give rise to an existential and ontological commitment, one hostile to any imaginative drifting from here to there?

My most general goal in this essay will be to lay the groundwork for calling into question these opposed presuppositions.

On the first side, I want to plead for a concept of the imagination that will highlight two traits that are usually misconceived by philosophy. First, imagination can be described as a rule-governed form of invention or, in other terms, as a norm-governed productivity. This is how Kant conceived imagination in his *Critique of*

* Translation by David Pellauer.

Judgment by coordinating the free play of the imagination and the form of the understanding in a teleology that had no goal beyond itself. Next the imagination can be considered as the power of giving form to human experience or, to take up again an expression I used in *The Rule of Metaphor*,/1/ as the power of redescribing reality. Fiction is my name for the imagination considered under this double point of view of rule-governed invention and a power of redescription.

Now turning to my other pole, the Bible, I would like in this essay to begin investigating two traits of reading that correspond to the two traits of the imagination just spoken of. As one part of this investigation, I would like to consider the act of reading as a dynamic activity that is not confined to repeating significations fixed forever, but which takes place as a prolonging of the itineraries of meaning opened up by the work of interpretation. Through this first trait, the act of reading accords with the idea of a norm-governed productivity to the extent that it may be said to be guided by a productive imagination at work in the text itself. Beyond this, I would like to see in the reading of a text such as the Bible a creative operation unceasingly employed in decontextualizing its meaning and recontextualizing it in today's *Sitz im Leben*. Through this second trait, the act of reading realizes the union of fiction and redescription that characterizes the imagination in the most pregnant sense of this term.

So this is the first presupposition of this essay, to seek *in* reading itself the key to the heuristic functioning of the productive imagination.

This presupposition, at first glance, may seem to set aside another way of approaching our subject that would consist in exploring the work of the imagination after reading, either as a personal form of the imagination — I have in mind Dorthee Sölle's fine little book *Imagination et Obéissance* — or as a collective form of the imagination — as in works on the relations between faith, ideology, and utopia, which I consider to be equally important. By placing myself at the very heart of the act of reading, I am hoping to place myself at the starting point of the trajectory that unfolds itself into the individual and social forms of the imagination. In this sense, my approach does not exclude this other wholly different approach but leads to it.

2. Within the vast domain of the form of the imagination at work in the biblical text, I propose to limit myself to one particular category of texts, the narrative texts. My reasons for this choice are as follows.

First, beginning from the side of a theory of fiction, I observe that today we possess a general theory of narratives, coming from literary semiotics, which may allow us to give a concrete meaning to the twofold idea of a rule-governed creation and a heuristic model. On the one hand, narratives may be seen as a remarkable example of rule-governed invention to the extent that their submission to narrative codes testifies to the encoded character of their invention, and where their abundance attests to the ludic character of this rule-governed generation. On the other hand, narratives offer a remarkable example of the conjunction between fiction and redescription. Narratives, in virtue of their form, are all fictions./2/ And yet it is through these fictions that we give a narrative form to our experience, be it individual or communal. Stephen Crites (1971: 291–311), in a noteworthy essay, has even spoken of "the narrative quality of experience" and shown how narrative provides a discursive articulation explicitly applicable to the narrative forms of lived experience.

Next, placing myself on the side of the biblical text, I can hardly be contradicted if I recall that there the narrative kernels occupy a central place and play an exceptional role from the election of Abraham to the annointing of David by way of the Exodus, and from the narratives of the life and teaching of Jesus to those of the Acts of the Apostles by way of the accounts of the Passion. Whatever may be the destiny of those narrative theologies that some thinkers are attempting to elaborate, these narratives may be for us a favorable occasion for making our first presupposition more precise, I mean that the act of reading should be seen as the meeting point of the itineraries of meaning offered by the text as a production of fiction (in the sense given above) and the free course (*parcours*) of meaning brought about by the reader seeking "to apply" the text to life. My second presupposition, therefore, will be that it is within the structure of the narrative itself that we can best apprehend this intersection between the text and life that engenders the imagination according to the Bible.

3. A further delimiting of my subject will follow from a third presupposition, namely that the narrative-parables (to use the terminology of Ivan Almeida [see below]) furnish the key to an enigma that I find H. Richard Niebuhr (1960) has perfectly outlined in his *The Meaning of Revelation*, the enigma of the passage from a narrative to a paradigm, which in turn governs the passage from a narrative to life, which is finally the heuristic character of

narrative fiction. Whitehead, whom Niebuhr quotes favorably, wrote in *Religion in the Making*, "Rational religion appeals to the direct intuition of special occasions, and to the elucidatory power of its concepts for all occasions."/3/ Niebuhr says of this,

> The special occasion to which we appeal in the Christian Church is called Jesus Christ, in whom we see the righteousness of God, his power and wisdom. But from that special occasion we also derive the concepts which make possible the elucidation of all the events in our history. Revelation means this intelligible event which makes all other events intelligible (p. 69).

But how does one intelligible event make other events intelligible? Here, between "our history" and that "special occasion," is interpolated the "rational pattern" Niebuhr calls an image: "By revelation in our history, then, we mean that special occasion which provides us with an image of which all the occasions of personal and common life become intelligible" (p.80).

It is no accident that Niebuhr develops this idea in a chapter entitled "Reasons of the Heart," which he opposes to the "evil imagination" evoked by Genesis. Yet his central affirmation seems to be more the formulation of a problem than the enunciation of a solution. How does a history or story become an image, a paradigm, a symbol for . . . (and not just a symbol of . . ., to take up a distinction of Clifford Geertz's [1973:118])? Niebuhr does do a good job in showing us the trajectory from history become an image to life, but he short-circuits the elevating of history to an image. Here is where a third presupposition intervenes, namely that the narrative parable is the type most favorable to investigating the link between a narrative and an image because the metaphorization process of a simple narrative is contained in the text itself by virtue of its literary form. To put it another way, the narrative-parable is itself an itinerary of meaning, a signifying dynamism, which transforms a narrative structure into a metaphorical process, in the direction of an enigma-expression (once again this is Almeida's term), the Kingdom of God, an expression that orients the whole process of transgression beyond the narrative framework while at the same time receiving in return a content of provisory meaning from the narrative structure. Here we may have, it seems to me, the most complete illustration of the biblical form of imagination, the process of parabolization working in the text and engendering in the reader a similar dynamic of interpretation through thought and action.

Someone may object, perhaps, that this third presupposition condemns us to taking as our paradigm one too narrow form of narrative, a form that we might even see as an exception rather than as exemplary. To show that the choice of narrative-parables is pertinent to our investigation of the biblical form of imagination, we would have to demonstrate that the operation of parabolization is not limited just to the narrative-parable, or that it does not appear here alone, but that it is implicitly at work everywhere else.

This is where a fourth presupposition comes in, a presupposition that will furnish the most restrictive delimitation of this inquiry but also the guiding thread of the whole study.

4. To ask what makes the narrative-parable a paradigm and not an exception, is to look for what makes the metaphorization at work in this type of narrative a process capable of other applications without becoming an interpretation that does violence to its text. In this essay, I have sought a key to this new enigma in an operation that the French structural school of text semiotics has brought to light, namely *intertextuality* or the work of meaning through which one text in referring to another text both displaces this other text and receives from it an extension of meaning.

Allow me to note that this recourse to the semiotics of texts does not imply any judgment, positive or negative, concerning the currently dominant method of historical-critical exegesis. It is a question of another technique which found its first application in the domain of fairy tales and folklore. (The historical-critical method itself is transposed from classical philology as applied to profane texts.) What is specifically different about the semiotic study of texts is that it does not ask about the history of redaction of a text or to what setting the successive authors of their respective audience might have belonged. Instead it asks how a text functions as a text in its current state. If one identifies exegesis with the historical-critical method, the semiotic analysis of texts is not a form of exegesis.

Yet in drawing upon the semiotics of texts, I find that I am not enclosing myself into structuralism's abstract combinatory devices. To the contrary, the notion of intertextuality will appear in what follows in this essay, not just as one complement to the structural analysis of narratives, but as an important corrective insofar as it dynamizes the text, makes meaning move, and gives rise to extensions and transgressions—in brief, insofar as it makes the text work.

A complete demonstration would include three steps. I shall only be able to develop the first one here.

The first step consists in showing that intertextuality is indeed the operation that assures the metaphorization of the simple narrative in the case of the parables. If this analysis is successful, I will have justified my third presupposition that the parable is not an exceptional literary genre, rather parabolization is a general procedure of the narrative form of imagination.

The second step would consist in showing that the restricted intertextuality, visibly at work in the case of the parables, works as well in the case of non-parabolic narratives. Two possible examples could be the intersection between narratives and laws in the Old Testament, and the over-all intersection between the Old and New Testaments. If this demonstration can be shown to be satisfactory, we shall have rejoined the conditions of the first Christian hermeneutic, which was effectively engendered by the intertextuality between "the one and the other testament," to use the title of a work by Father Paul Beauchamp. By passing in this way from the restricted intertextuality of the parables to the generalized intertextuality of the whole Bible considered as a single book, we may hope eventually to regain the level of our second presupposition that revelation is the transfer from *this* history to *our* history, as suggested by H. Richard Niebuhr.

Finally, the third step would consist in showing that this phenomenon of intertextuality, brought in this way to its highest level, is indeed the key to the rule-governed imagination which, by the privileged way of narrative, invites the reader to continue, on his or her own account, the Bible's itineraries of meaning. If this analysis can one day be carried through, we shall have recovered the level of our first presupposition that the biblical form of imagination is indivisibly a narrative and a symbolic form of imagination. By beginning this process today, while having in mind some notion of where we must go from here, we shall have begun to do justice to the second interpretation of the theme Dean Kitagawa has proposed, that of Dorothee Sölle in *Phantasie und Gehorsam* (1968), and that of those other authors who have worked on the relationships between faith, ideology, and utopia. But, as I have already indicated, the present essay is limited to showing the rootedness of the imagination (that comes after reading) in the imagination that is the very act of reading.

II. Intertextuality and Metaphorization in the Narrative-Parables

Why begin with the parables? Why not? By flattening out every text, semiotics gives me the right to begin from any fragment. This is how a *book* is made, it puts all its parts in synchrony, in a space that can be traversed in any direction, between the two covers, and beginning from any center. We shall reascend the succession of our presuppositions, therefore, by first applying ourselves to the fourth one that intertextuality is the key—or one of the keys—to the metaphorical transfer suggested by the famous clause: "The Kingdom of God is like . . ." I must admit that this aspect of the problem completely escaped me in my earlier work on the parables published in *Semeia* (1975: 29–148). I got trapped there by the question, "what makes us interpret the narrative as a parable?" I did not see the resources for responding to this question offered by the too easily overlooked trait that the narrative-parables are narratives within a narrative, more precisely narratives recounted by the principal personage of an encompassing narrative. Therefore I am going to try to show now by drawing on the work of Ivan Almeida, a professor at the Catholic University of Lyon, that the structure embedding one narrative in another narrative is the fundamental framework for the metaphorical transfer guided by the enigma-expression "Kingdom of God."/4/ The effect of this embedding is twofold: on the one hand, the embedded narrative borrows from the encompassing narrative the structure of interpretation that allows the metaphorization of its meaning; in return, the interpretant (to use an expression taken from C.S. Pierce) is also reinterpreted due to the feedback (*par choc en retour*) from the metaphorized narrative. Metaphorization, therefore, is a process at work between the encompassing narrative and the embedded narrative.

Therefore there are two errors to avoid in the interpretation of a narrative-parable: first, to consider only the primary narrative, neglecting its anchorage in another narrative; then one does not understand the phenomenon of metaphorization characteristic of the parable. Second, to reduce the parable to the speech act of the personage whose story is recounted in the encompassing narrative without taking into account the transforming action exercised by the primary narrative on the encompassing narrative. Of course we have learned from Jeremias's marvelous work on the parables that Jesus does something in telling the parables, but the parables in their turn are productive of meaning at the level of the narrative of the life of Jesus. We must understand therefore, says Almeida, not just "how this personage produces something with this narrative, but how this narrative produces something in the story of this personage" (p. 130).

To understand this work of meaning, we must first have taken into account the structures of the narrative following the semiotic method. My analysis presumes this analysis, but does not confine itself to it. Furthermore, it assumes that this analysis is done in a way that allows us to go further than ordinary structural analysis does, toward the transformation of the narrative-parable by the encompassing text. In what way? In a way that already notes the dynamism at work in the narrative in order to understand how this dynamism is transgressed by the embedding. To understand a narrative dynamically is to understand it as the operation of transforming an initial situation into a terminal situation. The most elementary function of a narrative, in this regard, is to account for this transformation. To read a narrative is to redo with the text a certain "line" or "course" (*parcours*) of meaning.

I stress this theme of a "course" which connotes the transforming dynamism of a narrative. In a way, it is the first form of imagination we encounter. A form of imagination incorporated into a transformation. A rule-governed form of imagination, encoded, yes, but authentically productive of meaning. It is because a narrative involves such a dynamism that it can be taken into the encompassing dynamism of the text within which it is embedded.

Not just any analysis of the primary narrative, consequently, can lend something to the work of metaphorization. Only the one that puts the accent on the course of meaning brought about each time by each parable. The phenomena of intersection are subsequently grafted on to those micro-universes where something happens, where something takes place.

I am adopting here A.-J. Greimas's model of analysis as used by Almeida. This is, as I said, a semiotic approach to texts completely distinct from the historical-critical method. It takes the text in its last state, just as it has been read by generations of believing and nonbelieving readers, and it attempts to reconstruct the codes that govern the transformations at work in the narrative. Such an analysis makes a semiotic organization appear in the narrative-parables that does not differ from the elementary grammar at work in popular folktales. This grammar is not uninteresting, however, if we know how to discern not just the paradigmatic character of these codes, as Lévy-Strauss does, but their *productivity*, that is, their aptitude for engendering transformations. In truth, the two aspects are linked, for if a code is a system of constraints—as are the phonological code, the lexical code, and the syntactical code at the level of *langue*—these constraints are at the same time the conditions for producing new narrative courses, just as the constraints of *langue* are also conditions for engendering new sentences. This is why the narrative form of imagination is both constrained and free at the same time.

I shall consider, as Almeida does, the example of two parables in Mark, the wicked husbandmen and the sower. Besides being the only parables common to the three synoptic Gospels, their position — the one near the beginning, the other near the end of that other course of meaning which, at the over-all level of the Gospel, is the incarnate word's march toward death — will constitute below an important indication of the intersection we are looking for between these two narrative-parables and the encompassing narrative.

1. The Narrative-Parable of the Wicked Husbandmen

Let us begin with "The Wicked Husbandmen." The personages are few in number: the vineyard owner, the tenants, and the successive envoys, the last of which is the son. An "object-value," the vineyard, circulates among them. To this must be added its fruits, which do not circulate, and though the owner sends for them it is in vain. The actions are also few in number, involving only a few verbs: to plant, hedge, rent, go, send, kill, etc. The actants, object-values, and segments of action make up a narrative insofar as a dynamism runs through all of them — from the planting of the vineyard to the refusal to hand over its fruits, from the departure of the owner to the murder of the son. We may represent this small drama as a conflict between two "narrative programs" (Greimas), that of the owner of the vineyard who wants to reap the fruits of the vineyard he has rented out, and that of the tenants who defeat this program. This dynamism, seen from the point of view of the owner, is a dynamism of progressive defeat. In semiotic terms, it is a dysphoric course, that is, one that fails to unite its subject to its object. As we shall see, the inverse case applies in the case of the sower.

But the semiotician does not stop here. He notes that this narrative takes place in relation to three stable themes which he calls isotopies, that is, semantic invariants.

The first isotopy is quite evident. It is the vegetation: vines, fruit, wine. More precisely, it is a vegetation-economic isotopy: a location, a harvest, an inheritance. This vegetative course from planting to fruit and the harvest will have its counterpart in a similar course in the parable of the sower, from the sowing to the harvesting of the grain. What they have in common, and what we have called and object-value, is an object with a dynamic, not a static value: it sprouts, grows, and does or does not bear fruit. The narrative transformation follows the potentialities of this object which Almeida characterizes as "an object with a surplus value" (*objet à plus-value*). What is more, it is these potentialities that release the quest that is the basis for the narrative: to go get some of the fruits. The whole narrative process may be summed up in a locution that is the theme correlative to the plot: from the initial lack created by the departure to the defeat of its redress.

The second isotopy is the one common to the actions of departing, sending, and above all fighting and killing. It concerns the life and death of a body. We shall not rediscover this isotopy in the sower where it will have been replaced by another isotopy which stands in a significant contrast to it—this will be the isotopy of the word.

The third isotopy is the one that runs the greatest risk of passing unperceived and that only a semiotic analysis can clearly recognize. It concerns the relations among places. The semiotician is attentive to it insofar as the narrative is a course. We will call it the spatial isotopy. Indeed, it is noteworthy that the entire continuation of the narrative from the sending of the first messengers to the murder of the last one—the son of the departed man—roughly constitutes a movement toward the inside of the enclosed vineyard. It is only within the enclosed vineyard that Mark has the son die. The dramatic movement from life to death is thus staked out by a spatial movement from outside where the owner has departed to, to inside where the son is killed./5/

Before turning to the second parable, let us already note the power of metaphorization initially contained in the three isotopies. Let us provisionally set aside the third isotopy, that of the places. It does not immediately reveal its metaphorical power. Particular attention must be paid to the places of Jesus' preaching and of his march toward death—from Galilee to Jerusalem, then to the Temple, then to the empty tomb—to register a similarity of movements from outside to inside. Louis Marin's (1971) work on the "Topic of the Passion" prepares us for the idea that the Gospel places are not geographical, that is, amenable to an empirical type of verification, but topological places, or, if one prefers, semanticized places which get their signification in relation to the dramatic course. In this sense, the spatial isotopy is not purely geometric. The places are capable of signifying more than just places for bodily movements. And in this sense, they are eminently metaphorizable./6/

As for the second isotopy, that of the body and death (Almeida's somatic isotopy), it is set in motion toward metaphorization by the text's conclusion: "And they tried to arrest him . . ." (Mk 12:12). Here the metaphorization plays directly between the content of the narrative (what is said) and its author (the speaker), who signifies himself through what he says. In other words, the destiny of the speaker is figured in what the narrative says./7/

As regards the first isotopy, that of the vineyard and its fruits, which we have called the vegetation-economic isotopy, the listener cannot miss its metaphorization that calls to mind Isaiah 5: "My beloved had a vineyard . . . . For the vineyard of the Lord of Hosts is the house of Israel . . . ." We can here catch a glimpse of how a narrative-parable is embedded in an encompassing narrative by means of the quotation that is the most explicit and most remarkable effect of intertextuality. Let us note in passing that this effect corrects the structuralist notion of an isotopy as a univocal level of discourse. Plurivocity is already present on the level of the primary narrative which is capable of being metaphorized.

The two beginnings of metaphorization that we have indicated, on the side of the body and on that of the vineyard, are also tightly interlaced with each other through the progress of the narrative. Something happens, in effect, in the narrative in that the tenants not only refuse to hand over the fruits but seize the first servant, beat him, and send him away empty-handed. The beaten servant is sent back *instead of* the requisite fruits. In this way, the dying body becomes the substituted and inverted sign of the refused object-value, the fruits of the vineyard. He is not just the owner's envoy, but detained *like* the refused fruits and sent back *in place of* them. "Like," "in place of," here is the beginning of a metaphorization that is inscribed as follows: so that the fruit may increase, life must decrease. We could speak here of an inverted metaphor. This rapprochement is a creation of the narrative which, at this moment, takes an odd turn. The messenger becomes something other than and more than a messenger, the "anti-metaphor" of the object-value, the fruit of the vineyard (p. 165). The seizing of the body occurs *in place* of the seizing of the fruits postulated by the logic of the narrative. The narrative form of imagination, which prepares the way for the metaphorical form, is already notable in this transgressing of the expectation created by the sending of the messenger who was supposed to seize some of the fruits, not be captured in his own body. The servant was sent empty-handed and returned "empty-handed" —as the text simply says —which makes an antithesis to the expected plenty from the harvest.

It is not just the isotopies in terms of which the acts are unfolded that can be metaphorized. The actants can also. Greimas distinguishes the most general actantial roles (subject, opponents, helpers) and their thematic investments—here a landlord, his sharecroppers, servants, and son. Each of these roles possesses a polysemy that makes possible, on the narrative plane, the explicit metaphorization through their context. Further, within the narrative itself, the man who planted the vineyard is revealed to be a father after having acted as the owner of the vineyard and the sharecroppers' landlord. At the same time, the vineyard goes from being simply the soil for producing fruit to an inheritance. It is the progression of the narrative that makes these successive investments of the actantial roles into their thematic roles take place. *Then* the sharecroppers posit themselves as substitute heirs: "Let us kill him, and the inheritance will be ours" (12:7). We could well speak here of the "odd logic" that guides this drama. In my earlier analysis of the parables in *Semeia*, I emphasized narrative extravagance as their common trait. It is through this narrative extravagance that the deceived landlord becomes a father who sends his son and thereby brings the narrative to its critical point, what Aristotle called the peripeteia which is answered by the denouement. In this case it is the refusal to recognize the son, his death in the vineyard, the interior that ought to have been the place of fructification and therefore of life: "And they took him and killed him, and cast him out of the vineyard" (12:8). The inside of the vineyard instead of being just a place is qualified by the action that occurs there. It is this action that makes the equation between the interior and death.

One last remark concerning the preparation, on the simple narrative plane, for the metaphorical transformations that are the principal object of our inquiry. The narrative ends with a segment outside the narrative (*un hors-récit*) where the listener is questioned: "What will the owner of the vineyard do? He will come and destroy the tenants, and give the vineyard to others" (12.9). This segment is outside the narrative first in the sense that the dysphoric climax is annulled by an action which is not spoken of as past, but which is posited as in the future as the response to a question. This action signifies the defeat of the defeat and the liquidating of the opponent. We shall see below how, in virtue of intertextuality, this postscript corresponds to the postscript to the whole Gospel. This segment is outside the narrative in the second place in the sense that it creates a new vis-à-vis to the master: "he will give the vineyard to others." At the same time, new roles for the master are created. These are not thematized but simply suggested by the indeterminateness of these "others."

As for the vineyard object-value which circulates among these actants, we do not know what it will produce once "given to others." Here the narrative, after having been closed on a definite defeat, is reopened to indefinite possibilities, thanks to the rhetorical device of the question, "what will the owner of the vineyard do?"/8/ By marking the intrusion of the narrator into the narrative through a summons addressed to the listeners, this question also marks the anchoring of the narrative-parable in the weft of the narrative that encompasses it and opens the way to the parabolization we are going to talk about. It marks this anchorage in another fashion by the allusion—which is equivalent to a quotation—to the parallel text of the "Song of the Vineyard" in Isaiah: "And now I will tell what I will do to my vineyard" (Is 5:5). In this way, the wicked husbandmen are again made ready to be metaphorized. If the one who "will come"—according to the postscript to the narrative—obliquely signifies the narrator himself, the wicked husbandmen begin to signify the listeners themselves: "for they perceived that he had told the parable against them" (Mk 12:12). But here we have already exited the narrative and taken the path of metaphorization. It has been helpful, I believe, to have seen how this metaphorical process is in a way woven into the narrative course.

The explicit metaphorization is further guided by the device of quotation in verses 10 and 11. At first, this quotation seems odd since it does not limit itself to evoking a defeat, or even the defeat of a defeat, but a victory with an "Easter" meaning: "This was the Lord's doing." This expression, placed at the hinge linking the narrative-parable and the encompassing narrative, designates the meaning vector of the entire metaphorical process, exactly as the enigma-expression "kingdom of God" does elsewhere. Now this quotation only functions to metaphorize what is outside the narrative if it contains symbolic resources that the quotation extracts from it. The quotation *transforms* the vineyard and its fruits (the vegetative isotopy) into a "head of the corner stone" (or architectural isotopy), by means of, may we venture to say, the whole entourage of stones in the course of the parable: the wine press in a pit, the surrounding and enclosing hedge, the tower that is erected. All these are terms that move from plant to stone. Whatever the case may be concerning this metonymic (press, enclosure, tower, corner stone) and metaphoric (the transfer from the vineyard to the head of the corner stone) game, it is capital that the signification wrested from the quotation is already a fact of intertextuality. Thanks to the criss-crossing between the narrative and the other texts, the vineyard—which is at stake in all the actions—does not stop signifying something more. Having been the bearer of fruits and an inheritance, it has become, on the spatial plane, the circumference within which, on the body plane, the murdered son's destiny is fulfilled. It is the narrative that extracts all this signifying power from the vineyard.

At the end of this analysis, we understand in what sense we could have said in beginning that the codes are not inert constraints but generate a structuring dynamism which is all ready for metaphorical transformation.

2. The Parable of the Sower

For the narrative-parable of the sower I will limit myself to those traits which, in a semiotic analysis, correspond to those of the parable of the wicked husbandmen. In this sense, we are entering into the process of intertextuality—the parables, in effect, should be read together. Together they constitute a universe of meaning in which the symbolic potentialities of one contribute, by means of their common context, to making the potentialities of another explicit.

A first inspection reveals a narrative process as euphoric as the preceding one was dysphoric. Its bearer is the very act of sowing with all its meaning potentiality that is connected with fecundity: planting, growing, yielding. This act of growing encounters three successive opponents: the birds, the sun, the thorns. The parable tells of the success of this operation despite three successive defeats. And the final success is itself drawn up in three ascending degrees: thirtyfold and sixtyfold and a hundredfold. All this is well known. The most interesting contribution of a semiotic analysis consists in the identifying of the planes of discourse or, in our vocabulary, the isotopies at play here. Here is where the most remarkable correspondences to the preceding parable spring forth.

It is clear that we again have the vegetative (or economic-vegetative) code of natural growth. The grain corresponds to the vines, eating to drinking. Do we also rediscover the spatial code? Its least significant occurrence is the progression from the periphery of the field to the good soil, which vaguely resembles the movement toward the inside of the course of the wicked husbandmen. More significant is the initial note: "Listen! A sower went out to sow." The field, understood as a whole, is the outside. It is this outside that is the place of the euphoric course.

But if we rediscover the two vegetative and spatial codes, we do not find the body and death code, represented in the preceding parable by the servants and son who are attacked and killed. What might correspond to it here? As the whole tradition has recognized, it is the word, that is, exactly the saying as projecting itself into what is said. This is what immediately makes the narrative a parable insofar as the metaphor which transports the fecundity of the grain into that of the word is inscribed in the narrative. The narrative in a way narrativized the fecundity metaphor. The text suggests this in different ways. First, through the immediate framing of the narrative: "*Listen!* A sower went out to sow" (4:3). "And he said, 'He who has ears to hear, let him hear'" (4:9). The Gospel of Mark puts this warning in Jesus' mouth, therefore in the encompassing narrative. It therefore ties it to the telling of the parable by attributing it to the speaker. The Gospel tells what Jesus tells. Several semioticians have emphasized the kinship of this procedure to that of *The Thousand and One Nights*. In the same way, the speaker signifies himself or herself as inside his or her narrative, and the same holds for the two groups designated as 1) "those who asked him concerning the parables" to whom Jesus declared, "To you has been given . . ."; and 2) those whom Jesus speaks about in saying "but for those outside . . ." (which implies that the first group is the "inside"). Through the feedback of this discourse by Jesus on the narrative, the first group, "you" (who are "inside"), is narrativized as being the actors of the euphoric process, the second group ("those outside") as the actors of the dysphoric process.

We shall return below to the complete sentence, "To you has been given the secret of the kingdom of God, but for those outside everything is in parables." It turns on the enigma-term "Kingdom of God," which belongs to the encompassing text and which introduces a new opposition between "the secret is given" and "everything is in parables," where "is in parables" signifies only in parables, that is, in an opaque figure, heard but not understood. That we have here a fact of intertextuality is underlined by the quasi-quotation of the Old Testament in the following verse: ". . . so they may indeed see but not perceive . . ." (cf. Is 6:9–19). This is a segment outside the narrative that the following verse (Mk 4:13) reinserts into the narrative weft through the use of a question: "Do you not understand this parable? How then will you understand all the parables?"

We see here how semiotic analysis differs from historical-critical exegesis which deliberately severs the explication that follows the parable from the parabolic narrative properly speaking, with the idea of isolating an original kernel that eventually would constitute the *ipsissima verba* of Jesus and risks ascribing the added explication to the redactors (and the ecclesial community they stem from). For semiotic analysis, the incorporation of the narrative and its interpretive commentary into one text is an irrecusable textual fact. So the task of this analysis is to disclose the isomorphisms between the narrative and the interpretation that contribute to the parabolizing of the narrative. It is the resemblance between the narrative courses (thirty, sixty, one hundred grains) on the one hand, and the sequence: understand, be converted, be forgiven, on the other. It is this isomorphism that allows the narrative's fiction to cross its borders and be oriented toward the enigma-expression, "Kindom of God," that polarizes it over-all. This effect is obtained through the criss-crossing of the vegetative and the verbal isotopies.

It appears, therefore, that the function of the sequence 4:10–13 is to insert into the meaning of what is said something about its being said and its reception. The destiny of the sowing which is lost three times, then which finally fructifies in abundance, is signified as the destiny of the very word (*parole*) that tells the narrative. A progression of abundance, similar to that of the grain harvest (thirtyfold, sixtyfold, a hundredfold), is indicated on the level of the diffusion of the terms "to understand," "to be converted," "to be forgiven." Thus the incomprehension of some — those "outside" — and the progress in understanding of others — "you" — is narrativized after the fact through the interpretation. To the extent that the destiny of the sowing is metaphorized as the destiny of the word, the destiny of the word is narrativized as the destiny of the sowing. This presupposes that what we have called the vegetative isotopy was not univocal. I mean, it was not just a question in the narrative of seeds and a harvest in the agricultural sense. A meaning potential in the language — that is, in the things already said — is liberated through the entangled twofold process of metaphorizing the narrative and narrativizing the metaphor.

Does not the same thing happen to the spatial isotopy (the outside of the field, its periphery, and its interior)? Between "those to whom the secret has been given" — a relation of intimacy — and those who remain "outside" — a relation of exteriority — the distance is no longer quantitative but qualitative. The euphoric process and the dysphoric process now depend upon these opposed values concerning proximity to the speaker of the word. Therefore these places are more than empirical sites and the degrees of distanciation are more than measurable distances. The spatial plane is itself also metaphorized insofar as the word is recognized as the "empty case" around which are organized the figures of this discourse (Almeida, p. 223).

It is this whole interplay, which is narrative and symbolic at the same time, that allows us to say that the word in the narrative-parable of the sower holds the same places as does the body in the narrative-parable of the wicked husbandmen./9/ This rapprochement that is also an opposition is authorized by the fact that the two other isotopies, the vegetative and the spatial ones, are common to the two narratives. And this inclines me to say that the vineyard in the first parable is to the sowing in the second what the inside in the first is to proximity in the second, and finally what the mortal body in the first is to the living word in the second. If we allow these rapprochements, a still more striking one proposes itself which will be the source of the great metaphor exhibited by the intersection of the two parables not just with each other, but with the principal narrative. We have said, in effect, that the narrative-parable of the wicked husbandmen has a dysphoric course and the narrative-parable of the sower a euphoric one. May we not say then that if the word is to increase, the body must decrease? This would be the great metaphor encompassing these two parables.

This recourse to context is therefore inscribed in the parable itself in two ways: on the one hand, on the side of what is said, through the metaphorical potentialities of the semantic fields that narrative semiotics encounters at the level of the narrative's large isotopies; on the other hand, on the side of the speaker, through the use of enigma-expressions such as "the secret of the kingdom of God" and "(only) in parables," which at the same time sort out the listeners and identify them respectively with the agents of the euphoric course (the fecundity of the sowing in the outside of the seeds) and the dysphoric course (the death of the body at the interior of the vineyard). The parable of the sower is exemplary in that it reunites these two processes, thanks to the exchanges between the speaking word and the spoken narrative. In this sense, it reveals the central operation by which the narrative becomes a parable.

3. Metaphorization through Intertextuality

We may now concentrate our attention on the second process, the metaphorization that occurs through the intersections of discourse within the encompassing narrative. It, more than any other, is what exercises the reader's productive imagination.

In sum, the whole meaning of my essay is contained here. A parable, the sower, contains in the perimeter of its pericope a first criss-crossing between the vegetative plane of fecundity and the more verbal one of communication of the message. This first criss-crossing produces the metaphor of a sown word or of a sowing that becomes a message. Then two parables taken together, the wicked husbandmen and the sower, created a second degree criss-crossing, this time within the micro-universe of the parables. This criss-crossing between the euphoric process of the word and the dysphoric process of the body's march toward death in turn prepares the way for a still more fundamental intersection between the two parables taken together and the narrative, which tells of the one relating the parable, that encompasses both. Finally, it is the same process of embedding that we try to follow in writings other than the Gospels, then between the Gospel and these other writings. In this series of embeddings, the same process of metaphorization is at work to guide the reader and to engender in him or her the capacity to pursue the movement of metaphorization beyond his or her reading.

Someone may object that, by saying this, I am abusing the notion of metaphor which, in classical rhetoric, only designates a transfer of the meaning of words. But I have shown in *The Rule of Metaphor* (1977: 65–100, 125–33) that the thought process of a metaphor has its initial support in the sentence, that is, in the operation of predication. A metaphor is first and essentially an "odd" predication that transgresses the semantic and cultural codes of a speaking community. The theory of intertextuality allows us to take another step and to call not just the collision between two semantic fields in a sentence a metaphor, but also an intersection between texts both of which carry their own semantic codes. The analysis of narrative-parables allows us to take this step and to extend the process of metaphorization to the widespread semantic conflicts instigated by the fact of intertextuality.

We may now approach by itself the phenomenon of parabolization through intertextuality that we have had to anticipate in order to account for the very dynamic of the narrative. I shall now take the two expressions parabolization and metaphorization as synonyms, it being understood that a metaphor can occur not only between words, but between whole sequences of sentences. The isotopies play a role at this discursive level comparable to that of the semantic fields that enter into interaction in metaphor-sentences. *Parabolization is the metaphorization of a discourse.* In the case of the narrative-parables, it consists of the metaphorization of a narrative taken as a whole. Intertextuality thus becomes an extension and, consequently, a particular case of the interaction I have placed at the center of my theory of metaphor. In this I follow I. A. Richards, Max Black, Monroe Beardsley, and others. These authors perceived that the semantic clash between significations does not occur without an interaction between contexts. It is this interaction that we are now going to consider.

The decisive point brought to light by Ivan Almeida is that the intersection among contexts is a phenomenon of *writing*. It is an operation of the *text* considered as a living work. Because the sequences have been written down together within the limits of one text — here a Gospel — they constitute a network of intersignification, thanks to which the isolated texts signify something *else*, something *more*.

This is how I understand the transition between semiotic explication and interpretation that has its fulfillment in the thought, action, and life of interpreting individuals and communities. We are leaving the structure (or sense), but we are not yet at the application or appropriation (the reference). We are accompanying *the interpretive dynamism of the text itself*. The text interprets before having been interpreted. This is how it is itself a work of productive imagination before giving rise to an interpretive dynamism in the reader which is analogous to its own.

I will limit myself here to sketching some of the relations of intertextuality through which our narratives, in becoming parables, give rise to a certain dynamism in the semantic sytem of the Gospel of Mark considered as a whole. We may arrange these procedures according to an increasing scale of intimacy in textual interaction and, consequently, in the synamization of one text to another. We will begin with (a) structural similarities between the englobing text and the embedded text. These isomorphisms are still external similarities compared to those we shall consider under (b) and (c).

The structural similarities play successively 1) on the contrast between the euphoric course and the dysphoric course in the two parables analyzed (placed respectively toward the beginning and the end of the Gospel); 2) on the interplay of isotopies sometimes common to the two parables (the vegetative and spatial isotopies), sometimes peculiar to each one (the corporeal isotopy in the one, the verbal isotopy in the other); and 3) finally on the explicit or implicit quotations which guide the references to other texts.

Beginning with the contrast between the euphoric and dysphoric courses, we can trace two homologous inverted courses on the level of the Gospel. Moreover, we can refer one to the *word* and the other to the *body*. In effect, what progressively happens in the Gospel is the *recognition* of Jesus as being the Christ. We can say in this regard that the Gospel is not a simple account of the life, teaching, work, death, and resurrection of Jesus, but the communicating of an act of confession, a communication by means of which the reader in turn is rendered capable of performing the same recognition which occurs inside the text./10/

This recognition, this knowledge concerning the narrator of the parables, progresses across the parables told by Jesus and about Jesus, his gestures and those ascribed to him, thereby engendering a sorting out of various groups: the crowd, adversaries, friends, and disciples who are thereby placed in variable relations of proximity to the person of Jesus. This sorting is aimed at constituting the community of those close to him who hear and understand.

This advance of the word is paralleled by a decline of the body, if we consider that the success of Jesus the miracle worker on the bodies of those he heals at the beginning of his ministry leads to the defeat of Jesus' body in death.

In this way, we see spring forth a certain parallelism between the over-all narrative structure of the Gospel and that of the two parables taken together. It is this parallelism instituted by the text—by the "texture" of the text—that makes a place for the process of mutual parabolization of the encompassing narrative and the embedded ones. This is the structural similarity that results from the mirror relation between the large and small narratives, apropos principally of the contrast between the euphoric course of the word and the dysphoric course of the body. The parable of the wicked husbandmen, in effect, simulates the dissemination and growth of the word. Perhaps here we should also refer to the transfiguration, the declaration before the High Priest, and the centurion's confession. The power of the metaphor is already present in this simple structural similarity where something *passes* from one text to another. A relation of intersignification is established between the large narrative and the small one. A new signification springs forth from this relation of intersignification as in the case of any live metaphor. The encompassing narrative and the embedded narratives seem to say together that the life of the word occurs through the death of the body.

The places, as we have seen, are also not foreign to this type of relation, both in the parables (the "outside" of the seeds, the "inside" of the vineyard) and in the encompassing narrative (the sending of the disciples, the empty tomb). In this regard, we must repeat again that the biblical places are eminently metaphorizable (the opposition between Galilee and Jerusalem is a semanticized space), and their metaphorization is promoted by the superimposition of relations of proximity between Jesus and another group of actors in the drama onto the properly spatial relations./11/

The text gives rise equally to a certain affinity between the theme of eating and drinking in the large narrative (the ears of grain plucked on the Sabbath, the miraculous multiplication of bread and fish, the bread and wine of the last supper), and the two parables' vegetative isotopy (the vineyard and the sowing). The superabundance of bread and fish miraculously multiplied, for example, is joined to the grain in the parable by means of the parallel metaphorization of both of them as a sign of the word which, in effect, is shared without being exhausted. We ought also not forget the leaven of the Pharisees and that of Herod (Mk 8:15) which become synonyms of the vineyard within which the son is killed by the wicked husbandmen.

(b) But parabolization is not reduced to an isomorphism that would leave the encompassing and embedded texts intact. The narrative-parable is not only the homologue of the large narrative, it signifies the destiny of the one who tells the parables and whose life is told by the Gospel. The exchange occurs between the personages of the embedded narrative and the person of the one who tells it. The bond between the encompassing narrative and the embedded narrative is made tighter here thanks to this remarkable trait of the narrative-parable that it is told by the personage of another narrative which encompasses it. Thus Jesus himself signifies the diminution of his mortal body in telling of the wicked husbandmen and he signifies the growth of his living word in telling of the superabundant fecundity of the grain.

In the same movement, the listeners are obliquely intended and analogously sorted out, following the models of the wicked husbandmen or the "bad" and "good" soil. (Let me remark in passing that this implication of the speaker in what is said in the narrative-parable in no way leads us back to the old discussions about Jesus' "messianic conscience." The problem is not psychological, but semiotic, in the sense that it is the belonging to one text and the work of the text as such that produce this reverberation of the narrative-parable on the person who tells it.)

(c) To the extent that the encompassing narrative and the embedded narrative penetrate each other, we catch sight of the role that enigma-expressions such as the "Kingdom of God" may play in this work of parabolization. The bond of these enigma-expressions, introduced by the encompassing narrative, to the immanent meaning of the narrative is infinitely more intimate than any isomorphism or even than any insertion of the illocutionary force of the utterance into the very weft of the spoken narrative. We may certainly still speak of an isomorphism to designate the correspondence we may observe between the enigma-expressions that the evangelist has put into the prologue which precedes the narrative of Jesus' ministry and into the epilogue of his ressurrection, expressions through which the kerygmatic meaning of the whole Gospel is anticipated (Son of God, Lord, Christ). It is a question, however, of much more than an isomorphism for we can no longer speak here of an isotopy in such expressions, even if we speak of a religious isotopy with the semioticians./12/ It is rather a question of limit-expressions, as I said in my article in *Semeia*, or, to use an expression of Jean Ladrière's (1975:116–41), of the horizon of structuration of the religious symbolism taken as a whole. If we may still speak of parabolization with regard to such limit-expressions, it is to the extent that a limit-expression's meaning, without being signified by any action or personage in a narrative, is signified by the movement of transgression that transports the narrative outside the customary logic of narratives. In this sense, the Kingdom of God is not what the parables tell about, but what happens in parables.

In my *Semeia* article, I attached this final process of parabolization to the aspect of the narrative's extravagance on the narrative plane. What landowner, in effect, would be so foolish as to send his son after his servants had been killed? What sowing could return thirtyfold, sixtyfold, a hundredfold? In this manner, the narrative metaphorizes itself by transgressing its own narrative structure through an "odd" usage of the art of narrating.

This metaphorizing relation runs in two directions. The expression "Kingdom of God" is in its turn referred to its enigmatic character by the movement of transgressing the narrative. Without this movement, these expressions risk falling to the rank of frozen religious representations. In this way, the expression "Kingdom of

God" left to itself, could become nothing more than a dead image with some vague political content. It is the extravagance of the narrative that, by bursting out of the mundane meaning of the narrative, attests that "my kingdom is not of this world," that is, does not belong to any specific project of human action and remains, in the strong sense of the word, impractical like some utopia. The expression-enigma, under the pressure of the extravagance of the narrative, thus becomes a limit-expression which breaks open the closed representations.

We have attained the point where it is no longer intertextuality as such that is at work, but where it is carried beyond itself by the meaning vectors of the enigma-expressions. To continue our analysis, it would be necessary to change methods and to show how these enigma-expressions mobilize in the reader opaque and mute expectations concerning liberation from evil and the regeneration of the "evil imagination." These limit-expressions, in effect, would be nothing more than hollow words if, on the one hand, human beings did not have some experience of limit-situations such as evil and death and the strong desire to be freed from them. It is these fundamental experiences that the enigma-expressions come *to configure*. But they would still only be words, if, on the other hand, they were not preceded by religious representations borne (*charriées*) by an older culture which these limit-expressions come to correct. It is the task of hermeneutics to correlate what these limit-expressions intend with human experience in its religious quality and with the available representations already qualified as religious by our culture. In brief, it is in configuring the most tenacious and most dense human hope, and by rectifying traditional religious representations, that limit-expressions continue their course beyond a narrative. As Almeida says, we leave the structural analysis of isolated sequences for the interpretation that is at work in the text as a whole. We are now leaving the interpretation internal to the text for a hermeneutic of the text's *referential intentionality*. But the passage from the text to life, which governs the passage from the semiotic phase of interpretation to its existential phase, is still guided by something that takes place in the text which, with Ladrière and Almeida, I have called the text's horizon of structuration. The new configurations of people's religious experiences and the rectifications of their representations are still accompanied by the new restructuration that the expression-enigma "Kingdom of God" and others similar to it impose on the signifying dynamism working in the narrative-parables. In short, it is still the parabolizing of the narrative, brought to its highest degree of incandescence, that gives rise to the transition from semiotic interpretation to existential interpretation. Here is where we pass from the work of imagination *in* the text to the work of imagination *about* the text.

And here is where our inquiry guided by the idea of intertextuality must end, at least for the moment.

NOTES

/1/ Ricoeur (1977:216–56).

/2/ Metz (1966:333–43). "Tout récit a pour conséquence immédiate d'irréaliser la chose racontée."

/3/ Niebuhr (1960:69), quoting Alfred North Whitehead, *Religion in the Making* (Cleveland: The World Publishing Company, 1960), p. 31.

/4/ Almeida (1978:117). He defines a parable as follows: "Un récit-parabole est un récit raconté par un personnage d'un autre récit qui l'englobe."

/5/ I will set aside that to which structural semiotics attaches the most importance, the possibility of representing every narrative maneuver on a semiotic square. I am somewhat doubtful about Almeida's thesis (p. 169) that, "through a whole series of narrative 'maneuvers' which might appear to us to be aleotory, an implacable semantic logic is expressed through the determining of the courses that the transformation algorithm will be forced to follow." I am much more attentive to the fact that it is because the narrative does follow a certain course that we can *after the fact* project the poles, the axes of contrariety, the schemes of contradiction, and the relations of implication onto an immobile figure. In any case, it is more important to note that in the series of messengers there is a progression to the inside of the vineyard than to stop with the fixed polarities of its movements. The second servant in this sense signifies *more* than the first one and the son *still more* in this two-fold progression on the planes of the body and space. If it is true that the narrative course is inscribed on the figure of the semiotic square, it is on the condition that the narrative *advances* and constitutes a *course*. The course, in this sense, engenders the structure.

/6/   "As has been said, the places function in the text as a semantic element not determined by the dictionary but easily contaminated. They are impregnated with significations left to them by the transforming actions and thus serve to fix the semantic continuity of the sometimes disparate events" Almeida (1978:178).

/7/   Almeida (1978:166) is willing to recognize that we cannot reach the end of a structural analysis here without anticipating the metaphorical effects. Conversely, he is correct to emphasize "the structural condition of this movement of metaphorization."

/8/   It is here that structural analysis runs the greatest risk of leaving aside what is essential. By projecting all the courses on the famous semiotic square, it requires them to satisfy a logic that closes the square. The liquidating of the opponent gives the diagram "the course that the square lacked" Almeida (1978:188). I would emphasize instead that it is the interplay of metaphors that, by producing meaning, allows the square to be closed and that gives the semiotician the conspicuous satisfaction of having "buckled up the semantic course" (ibid.). Yet can we, within the same system, both close the square and open the narrative to something outside the narrative? The distinction borrowed from Greimas between the topical narrative and a correlated narrative conceals the difficulty rather than resolving it.

/9/   I am hesitant about calling this plane of the word an isotopy in the same sense those of space and vegetation are. To the extent it is the "empty case" and only narrativized after the fact, we may not consider it an isotopy belonging to the narrative itself, something Almeida does not recognize sufficiently.

/10/   We could consider as the encompassing narrative in relation to the narrative-parable the narrative of the days of Jesus' life that end in his passion and death, therefore from the calling of the disciples to the women's fear at the tomb. We could then take as adjoined narratives ("correlated" narratives in A.-J. Greimas's sense), the framing narratives throughout which the text posits and in a way proposes in advance the meaning that the narrative properly speaking must produce, the prologue Mk 1:1–13, the epilogue Mk 16, along with the sequence on the death of John the Baptist (Mk 6:14–29) which anticipates the meaning of Jesus' death. This is why I speak of recognition to designate the confession professed by the very personages in the Gospel narrative, culminating in the centurion's confession. The narrative of the life and death of Jesus is organized in such a way that the knowledge unveiled right at the beginning should be appropriated by the actors themselves and, beyond them, by the reader. It is the work of the text to do this.

/11/ Let me recall again my doubt concerning the possibility of a structural analysis independent of these implicit or explicit processes of metaphorization. In effect, the isotopies are immediately and directly metaphorized. It is only through an abstraction that we constitute them as isotopies, that is, as univocal levels of discourse.

/12/ Here I disagree with Ivan Almeida who, to remain as long as possible in accord with Greimas's structural analysis, extends the categories of that analysis into a region of meaning where we can decidedly no longer speak of an isotopy in the rigorous sense of the term. If, as the author so well puts it, these expressions are *expressions-énigmes*, they do not designate any determined object, but the horizon of structuration, the dynamizing pole, the vanishing point of the whole process of parabolization. Consequently, we may no longer speak of an isotopy, which would assume the stability of one theme running through all the relevant terms of a single semantic field. This is why I hesitate to speak of a "religious isotopy" in the sense we have spoken of a vegetative, spatial, and verbal isotopy. Indeed, we have already seen the notion of an isotopy vacillate due to the effect of metaphorization which affects almost all the terms of a narrative-parable.

WORKS CONSULTED

Almeida, Ivan
1978   *L'Opérativité sémantique des récits paraboles. Sémio-
               tique narrative et textuelle. Herméneutique du dis-
               cours religieux.*

Crites, Stephen
1971   "The Narrative Quality of Experience." *Journal of
               the American Academy of Religion* 39:291–311.

Geertz, Clifford
1973   *The Interpretation of Cultures.* New York: Basic
              Books.

Ladrière, Jean
1975   "Le Discours théologique et le Symbole." *Revue
              des Sciences Religieuses* 59:116–41.

Marin, Louis
1971   *Sémiotique de la Passion: topiques et figures.* Paris:
              Bibliothèque de Sciences religieuses.

Metz, Christian
1966   "Remarques pour une phénoménologie du narra-
              tif." *Revue d'Esthetique* 19:333–43.

Neibuhr, H. Richard
1941   *The Meaning of Revelation.* New York: The Mac-
              Millan Co. Reprinted, 1960.

Ricoeur, Paul
1975   "Biblical Hermeneutics." *Semeia* 4:29–148.

1977   *The Rule of Metaphor: Multidisciplinary Studies of
              the Creation of Meaning in Language.* Trans.
              Robert Czerny. Toronto: University of Toronto
              Press.

Sölle, Dorothee
1968   *Phantasie und Gehorsam.* Stuttgart: Kreuz-Verlag;
              English translation: *Beyond Mere Obedience: Re-
              flections on a Christian Ethic for the Future.*
              Trans. W. Denet. Minneapolis: Augsburg,
              1970.

THE WILLIAM RAINEY HARPER CONFERENCE ON BIBLICAL STUDIES

Lecture and Seminar Schedule

Wednesday,
October 3

Swift Lecture Hall

8:00 P.M.

Keynote Address

Welcome: Joseph M. Kitagawa, University of Chicago

Introduction: Hans Dieter Betz, University of Chicago

"The Bible as a Document of the University"
Gerhard Ebeling, University of Zurich

Thursday, October 4
10:00 A.M.

2:00 P.M.

Seminars

"The Bible and the Hermeneutical Task"
John Dominic Crossan, DePaul University

"The Hebrew Scriptures as a Source for Moral Guidance"
Sheldon Blank, Hebrew Union College

"The Bible and the Imagination"
Paul Ricoeur, University of Chicago

"The Bible and Civil Ordering and Reordering"
John Howard Yoder, University of Notre Dame

Swift Lecture Hall
8:00 P.M.

Keynote Address

Welcome: Martin E. Marty, University of Chicago
Introduction: Samuel Sandmel, University of Chicago

"The Bible as a Document of Believing Communities"
James Barr, Oxford University

Friday, October 5
10:00 A.M.

1:30 P.M.

Swift Lecture Hall
3:30 P.M.

Seminars

"The Bible and the Understanding of Humankind"
Phyllis Trible, Union Theological Seminary

"The Canon as the Source for Preaching and Worship"
David Bartlett, University of Chicago

"The Bible and Theology"
David Kelsey, Yale University

"Retrospective Reflections on the Bible as Document for University and Believing Communities"
Hans Dieter Betz and Samuel Sandmel, University of Chicago

78 / WILLIAM RAINEY HARPER CONFERENCE

All sessions of the conference are free and open to the public.

We gratefully acknowledge the patronage of the Lilly Endowment, Inc. in making this conference possible.

Other scheduled conference participants included: David Aune, Joseph Blenkinsopp, John Burkhart, Edward Campbell, O.C. Edwards, Jr., Earle Hilgert, Robert Jewett, Robert Karris, Eugene LaVerdiere, George Nickelsburg, Carolyn Osiek, Malcolm Peel, David Reeves, Robert Scharlemann, Robin Scroggs, Jonathan Z. Smith, Graydon Snyder, Bastiaan Van Elderen, Bruce Vawter, Roy Ward, Raymond Williams.